Parenting
with
Purpose

Other Books by Lynda Madison, Ph.D.

*Keep Talking: A Mother-Daughter Guide
to the Pre-Teen Years*
(Andrews McMeel Publishing, 1997)

Parenting
with
Purpose

Progressive Discipline
from Birth to Four

Lynda Madison, Ph.D.

**Andrews McMeel
Publishing**
Kansas City

www.andrewsmcmeel.com

98 99 00 01 RDH 10 9 8 7 6 5 4 3 2 1

Library of Congress Cataloging-in-Publication Data

Madison, Lynda.
    Parenting with purpose : progressive discipline from birth to four / Lynda S. Madison.
        p.   cm.
    ISBN 0-8362-6768-0 (pbk.)
    1. Toddlers—United States—Psychology.   2. Parenting—United States.   3. Child rearing—United States.   I. Title.
    HQ774.5.M33   1998
    649'.1—dc21   98-19803
                                                                CIP

The views expressed herein are not necessarily those of the staff or management of Children's Hospital, Omaha.

This book is intended to provide information for educational purposes only. The suggestions for managing childhood behavior should not take the place of the advice of a physician or child psychologist who knows your child personally.

The individuals depicted in this book are composite characters drawn from my life experiences and client contacts. Any resemblance to real individuals is purely coincidental. The circumstances presented are real, but names and other identifying information have been changed to conceal actual identities.

To Jim, my husband and friend,
and my lovely daughters, Megan and Audrey.

Acknowledgments

I have many people to thank for their support, advice, and encouragement as I prepared this book. I offer my gratitude to the following readers: my parents, Elvira and Max Sallach; Carla Ketner, M.A.; Steve Waszak, M.B.A.; Kim Masters; Kent Kronberg, M.D.; Mary Fran Flood, Ph.D.; Ann Matzke, M.S.; Michael Moran, M.D.; Natalie Gendler, Ph.D.; and Michael Neise, Ph.D. I appreciate the support of my agent, Frank Weimann, and my editor, Jake Morrissey. And I am especially grateful to my husband, Jim, for many hours of listening, reading, and offering input—and for doing more than his share to keep our house in order as I worked to get this book in print.

Contents

Contents

Contents

Parenting
with
Purpose

PART I
Parenting with Purpose

Keep Tomorrow in Mind

RECENTLY I SAT WAITING for my husband and daughters on a bench at a shopping mall. Approaching my perch from three stores away was a large man in a business suit complete with white shirt and red tie. He walked quickly, pushing a stroller that held a pudgy blond toddler who was trying his best to escape the entrapment. As the boy leaned over the side of the stroller, his seat belt held him in, and he twisted around to reach for his father. The man's mouth drew into a frown as he quickened his pace toward my observation post. Plopping down next to me, he let out a sigh that told of a hard day at the office and a frustrating shopping trip. He turned the stroller sharply around to face his child, and I wondered what he might do. To my considerable surprise, he leaned his face close to his son, spoke softly to him at first, and then made a series of ridiculous faces that caused the boy to squeal with delight. In response, the man laughed a deep, hearty guffaw and escalated his one-man show: He tickled the boy's nose, ruffled his hair, and pretended to grab his nose between two knuckles, then hide it in his pocket. The scene was so captivating that I laughed right along with them. Turning toward me, the boy held out his hand, apparently considering my nose as a possible addition to the game.

"Fun, aren't they?" I said wistfully, honestly. I was surprised at the tightness in my throat and the tear that pooled in my eye. I wouldn't trade a minute of my life as mother of the two preteen girls off looking for three-ring notebooks and school clothes, but for a moment I felt a little pang of sadness as I remembered just how much fun their early years had been. Toddlers, I thought, are ready-made entertainment: They can get anyone to act like Robin Williams. Their giggles, their antics, are captivating. Everything they do spawns brag books, photo albums, and happy talk with utter strangers.

I searched the mall for other touches of nostalgia, and my eyes focused on a small boy just a little older than the one in the stroller. His parents were steering him through the throng of shoppers, each holding one of his hands. They were headed for the door marked "Parking Lot" when the boy caught sight of a plastic amusement horse a few benches from me. As his parents coaxed him away, he cried and kicked, then sat defiantly on the floor between them. Their efforts to get him to stand up failed miserably, and the couple exchanged looks of exasperation and shook their heads. Finally, the man boosted the boy onto the horse and plunked a quarter into the slot. This silenced the young cowboy, and he sat happily—until the ride ended. Then the tantrum started all over again. This scene gave me the same jolt I get when the phone rings during my favorite part of a movie. My heart rate quickened, the tear in my eye dried up, and I no longer felt like laughing. I remembered that although toddlers are fun, they take truckloads of energy and patience.

Most parents know that child rearing is not going to be easy: They expect messy diapers, sleepless nights, and tantrums. However, not everyone is ready for the challenge toddlers present. Young children sometimes refuse to get dressed, they pull things out of drawers, and they scream in the middle of the grocery store. They whine and beg for toys and candy, and they crawl under tables at restaurants. Situations like these can make anyone feel helpless. They frustrate even the calmest of parents, making them want to hide from others who are watching them "manage" their kid. Every toddler throws surprises at her parents, and every parent has moments of doubt. It boils down to how often one wants to experience them. Everyday toddler behaviors become more extreme and more frustrating when parents aren't prepared for them—or if they respond inappropriately. It helps to know what to expect and how to respond when difficult situations arise.

Parents want their children to grow up to be confident, happy, independent adults. They want their sons and daughters to learn to make good choices, respect others, and be treated well in the world, and they want them to have more opportunities than they had themselves. These goals are admirable and wise, but easy to lose sight of when you are dealing with messy hands and food on the floor. At times the only goals that seem to matter may be getting to work on time, cleaning up the kitchen, or getting the noise to stop. Good parents occasionally raise their voices or act childish in a frustrating situation, and isolated, minor events like this don't automatically ruin their child's chance of becoming a competent adult. But if parents develop a regular pattern of these behaviors, they color their child's perception of them and the world. Children learn from their parents how to treat other people. *The way you act when you are under stress is every bit as important to your child as the fun times you have in the park.* If you show excessive anger, resentment, or guilt at the annoying things your child does, you will do a disservice to your child and your parenting goals. Your reactions to tantrums, bedtime problems, and frustrating shopping trips set the stage for years of interactions with your child.

The purpose of this book is to help you think about and develop your parenting style. You should feel confident that your everyday behaviors, although they will not be perfect, facilitate the long-term goals you have in mind for your child. *That means thinking about the purpose of your parenting rather than concentrating your energy on the procedures you will use to manage behavior.* You are most likely to parent successfully if you think about your goals and philosophy and understand the *rationale* behind various discipline techniques. The patterns of interaction you develop early with your child can make parenting a wonderful experience. *Planning* your reactions to her behaviors as she grows and develops can prevent many problems later in life.

This book does not offer a quick-fix approach to parenting. Rather than presenting isolated techniques for addressing problem behaviors, it leads you through exercises designed to help you clarify your parenting goals and philosophy. The first two sections of the book focus on the foundations of effective parenting. Part III explains the rationale behind fundamental discipline methods and helps you integrate behavioral principles with an overall philosophy of parenting with purpose. The final section applies specific techniques to specific problem situations. Even in this more how-to part of the book, there is an emphasis on thinking about your parenting philosophy, knowing your goals in using discipline, and selecting techniques that are consistent with them. By reading the book in this sequence, you will develop a parenting approach that is *proactive* rather than *reactive*—and use discipline that has reason and purpose.

How Problems Start

A YOUNG COUPLE recently brought their six-year-old son to see me. Jason was a large, muscular first-grade boy with freckles and a complexion that matched his red hair when he became angry. According to his parents, he was angry all the time, and they argued with each other about how to discipline him. He was unruly at school, fought on the playground, and back-talked at home.

"I can't stand his attitude," said his mother. "I ask him to do something and he tells me to shut up. I do everything for him, and he can't find the time to tell me good morning."

Jason's father was equally disgusted. "He was trouble from the start," he said, "always wanting his own way. He's never going to amount to anything if he keeps this up." Neither parent could think of a good thing to say about Jason, yet both of them had come to see me because they wanted help for their son.

As a psychologist, I have heard the concerns of parents for over sixteen years. Their problems have all been unique, but, except for some terribly abusive individuals, all the parents I met had good intentions for their children. Many of them had basically normal children whose problem behaviors began long before they entered school.

Jason's certainly did. From early childhood he and his parents were off on the wrong foot. Mr. and Mrs. Jones complained about bedtime problems, temper tantrums, and broken toys, and they rarely agreed about parenting. Their approach changed frequently, too. They varied their rules and discipline techniques so often that Jason never knew who was going to do what to him next. These parents established a problematic relationship with their son very early in his life.

Jason's parents weren't completely to blame. He had a difficult temperament even as an infant. Worn down by their son's challenging personality and high activity level, his parents were understandably confused and distressed about how to manage his behavior. Difficult work schedules and financial pressures meant their attention to parenting was limited, and they had no family nearby to offer support. Mrs. Jones read one magazine after another looking for tricks of the trade, and both parents found themselves trying various approaches without knowing why they used them or what to expect. Getting no lasting results, they convinced themselves that nothing worked. Every tantrum or bedtime struggle told them they had failed, and they were angry with Jason and each other. Now, with Jason in the first grade, the situation was clearly out of control. Had Mr. and Mrs. Jones thought about their philosophy when Jason was young, their discussions might have led them to seek advice, choose a single, consistent approach, and feel more confident and proud as parents. Had they understood more about discipline, they might have prevented many of the problems Jason was facing.

How Do You Spell Success?

I HAVE KNOWN MANY children with problem behaviors, and even more who are well behaved. No doubt a variety of factors contributed to the way these children turned out, some of which had nothing to do with their parents. Nevertheless, over many years, I have noticed that parents who succeed in raising well-behaved, responsible children have certain vital qualities in common. *These qualities are commitment, trustworthiness, respect, and good technique.*

No parent has equal amounts of these four qualities. You can be totally *committed* to being a good parent but not know how to respond to a tantrum. You can be completely *trustworthy* and not want to put forth the effort it takes to practice and use appropriate discipline techniques. And you can know all about discipline *techniques* but not apply them in an atmosphere of basic *respect* for your child. When parents ignore any of these ingredients, they seriously decrease their chances of achieving their parenting goals. Shortchanging them makes managing a young child's behavior more difficult and creates bigger and more serious power struggles down the road.

What exactly is successful parenting? Most parents would agree with the long-term goals of raising their children to be confident, happy, independent adults—adults who make good choices and respect others as well as themselves. Unfortunately, adulthood is a long time for parents to wait to know if they are doing it right. Personally, I need a shorter-term way to measure whether I am progressing toward these ultimate goals. For me, success does *not* mean raising children who *never* argue with each other or their parents. It does *not* mean having a toddler who *never* bites or a preschooler who *never* throws tantrums. And it does *not* mean *always* being sure of your actions or choice of words.

Successful parenting means having basically happy children who are truly fortunate to live with you—not because of the *things* you provide them, but because of the way you *feel* about them and *act* toward them. It means being able to drift off to sleep most nights thankful for the opportunity to parent and proud of the way you have treated your children. It means hoping that they will learn to treat others, including you, the same way. It requires that you respond to your child's behavior in a way that teaches him how to solve problems and how to win your approval—not just how big and strong you are. And it means giving a lot of approval. Successful parenting depends on your commitment, trustworthiness, respect, and good technique. These qualities lay an essential foundation upon which your child can grow to be well behaved, trustworthy, and respectful in return—and more likely to learn from and succeed in the world. Having them in your parenting style may sound like a lofty ideal; after all, no one is perfect. However, on the whole I think it is important to strive to fill one's life with these ingredients, as a person and as a parent. They are present in the lives of all the people I know who are successful in either category. *You may not think about these ingredients as you manage a tantrum or clean pudding off the wall, but your success as a parent depends on your ability to incorporate them into just such everyday acts.*

◆ List four qualities you value most in your friends. Are they the ones you would like your child to have when he or she becomes an adult?

◆ What characteristics have you seen in other parents that you would like to have? What did they do that showed these particular qualities?

◆ How will you know if you are doing a good job as a parent?

PART II

Key Ingredients
of Successful Parenting

Commitment

What Children Need

EVERY CHILD HAS BASIC physical needs that must be met in order to survive to adulthood—food, shelter, and safety—but for children to develop into successful, happy adults, they must also have a basic *emotional* need met: the need for security. *Being emotionally secure when you are a child means having at least one provider you can count on to consistently love, value, and encourage you, no matter what happens.* Children who do not have this kind of security have a harder time loving, trusting, and valuing others, and themselves, even when they become adults. Although some of them eventually overcome the adversity of feeling disregarded and unimportant, it is not without a price. Many go through years of unhappiness and confusion before coming to peace with their backgrounds. As a parent, you must create a secure environment for your child when he or she is very young if you want to offer your child the best chance of becoming an emotionally healthy adult.

Successful parents gradually help their children learn to meet their own needs, but this job takes years of effort. Parents must start out meeting their children's needs for them; if they don't, their children react in some way—not on purpose, but usually not positively, either. It is easy to tell when a child's physical needs aren't met; they cry or beg or become too thin.

But an unmet need to be loved, valued, or encouraged is not so obvious. When a child's need for security is not met, the child may withdraw, become angry, act out, or exhibit any number of other behaviors that can easily be mistaken for misbehavior. *If you don't attend to your child's emotional needs, these behaviors will increase and require even more of your attention. If you respond with anger or frustration, you will create unhealthy ways of interacting with your child that will lead to future battles and disappointment.*

A few months ago, a couple approached me after one of my presentations; a nice-looking man and woman who carried a lovely little girl with huge brown eyes. They told me Katie was two, their only child, and that she was incredibly whiny and clingy. I agreed to meet with them but asked them not to bring Katie along so we could discuss their concerns alone. A week later, when I greeted the couple in my waiting room, I was surprised to see Katie with them. The dark-haired girl sat quietly in her mother's lap holding a stuffed bear. She eyed me suspiciously when I spoke to her, then buried her head in her mother's coat.

"Katie won't be any trouble," the mother explained. "She'll sit quietly while we talk, won't you, Katie?" Katie did not uncover her face.

I explained that I am not comfortable talking about children, even little ones, in front of them; there are too many adult words and feelings they don't understand. But when I suggested that I talk to the parents one at a time, they disagreed about whom should leave the room first.

"She won't stay with you," said Mrs. Green to her husband. "Besides, I think *I* should tell about Katie's problems. I know her better than you."

"That's because she never leaves your side," he said. "That's why we're here, remember?"

"If you were home more often, maybe she'd know you better," said the mother, speaking louder than necessary.

Mr. Green rose to his feet. Katie lifted her head from her mother's shoulder, her dark eyes shining with tears as she looked back and forth between the two adults. She whimpered as Mr. Green topped his wife's volume. "Someone has to make a living around here. Maybe you should get a job instead of coddling her all the time."

I intervened just as Katie started to cry. "Your discussion seems to be upsetting Katie," I suggested. I took a box of crayons and some paper from my desk. "Next time you come let's discuss what you expect and need from each other. For today, let's try to reassure Katie that things are okay." I sat down; so did the Greens. Katie eyed the crayons but didn't move. "Mr. Green, why don't you draw a face for Katie?" Mr. Green looked annoyed, but drew a face. "What about you, Mrs. Green?" Katie climbed off her lap when her mother began to draw, then took a crayon her father offered and made some marks on the paper. As we talked about when the parents could return, Katie began to relax and explore the office. Mr. and Mrs. Green scheduled a second appointment and promised to leave Katie with a relative.

At the next session the Greens began to discuss some of their conflicts over their roles in the family—and to see the connection between Katie's behavior and their own. They had difficulty keeping Katie away from their marital quarrels, which threatened her sense of security. Katie had finally attached herself so desperately to her mother that it became a problem for her parents. Mr. and Mrs. Green began to realize that they had lost sight of considering what Katie needed, which is a key element of commitment.

Put Your Needs Where They Belong

The Greens' arguments about finances and responsibilities clearly showed that adults have some of the same needs their children have. Physically, they need food, shelter, and safety, and they must have a way to insure those things will continue to be available. They must find housing, earn money, manage a budget, arrange for childcare, buy groceries—the list goes on and on. In addition to caring for these physical needs, adults need emotional security much like children. They need to feel valued by others, belong to a support system of family and friends, and have vital and supportive partnerships with people they love. They want to feel good about their ability to carry out the roles they have assumed—such as employee, spouse, or parent—and encouraged by the people who are important to them.

Satisfying all these needs for oneself can be a struggle. Earning money, managing a budget, and seeking supportive relationships can add stress to anyone's life. Raising children makes it even more difficult. Children mean more roles to juggle, more mouths to feed, and more people to please. Children can strain a budget, worry parents who are already anxious, and restrict the activities of those who want a social life. Sometimes parents see their children's needs as just one more obstacle to meeting their own. A child who screams in response to a request or tears up a valuable document can seem like a threat to a parent whose self-esteem is already suffering. It can feel as if the whole world is there in a two-foot-tall person, sticking out its tongue and defying control. When people do not respond to you the way you want them to, it is easy to feel unimportant. When the person is your child, it is easy to jump to the conclusion that you are an ineffective parent.

Adults with personal problems can have a hard time noticing their children's needs; they can easily dismiss signs of insecurity like Katie's whining and clinging to her mother. Parents who are distracted by their own needs can find the needs of others frustrating and misinterpret their child's behaviors as intentionally adding to their stress. When parents don't respond or respond inappropriately, they begin interaction patterns that can lead their child to poor problem-solving, poor social relationships, and noncompliance with adults.

Children always complicate the lives of parents who have unmet needs of their own. However, in the midst of the struggle to fulfill their own lives, parents must find ways to provide for their children. Otherwise, they cannot achieve the ultimate goal of raising their children to be confident, happy, independent adults. *Parents have the responsibility to meet their child's basic needs without being asked—and without thanks—even though it means putting their own desires on hold for a while.*

Of course, adult needs are important, and they must be addressed at some level in order for parents to be emotionally available to their children. The key to remember is that your needs are not your child's business. It is your responsibility to make sure they do not *become* your child's business, overtly or covertly. There will be times when your needs must wait until you can arrange time away from your child to deal with them. If you share your distress or insecurity with your child, you will create distress and insecurity for him or her, and ultimately more problems and distress for yourself. When you meet your child's needs first, you avoid compounding your own. To parent successfully with the future in mind, you must avoid causing your child to feel—and behave—insecurely.

Meeting your child's needs ahead of your own does not require mindless self-sacrifice. On the contrary, it is a very rational process. First of all, your child can't meet even his most basic needs at this age. Second, as an adult you have the maturity and judgment that allows you to put off satisfaction when it is important. Third, by taking care of your child, you *are* taking care of yourself, making the best possible future for your child and for you as a parent. Finally, you have the ability to separate needs from wants. Your child won't reach this stage for many years.

The distinction between *needs* and *wants* is an important one; children and even parents often confuse the two. As a simple example, you can *need* food because you are hungry or *want* it simply because it tastes good, but they are not the same thing and do not deserve equal effort. You can want a new car even though your old one works perfectly well. Of course, getting something you want just because you want it is not always a bad thing—unless it interferes with satisfying your more basic needs or, more important, those of your child. A child *needs* food, shelter, and safety if he is to survive to adulthood; he *needs* to be loved, valued, and encouraged in order to be competent and productive. His needs should come before anything else. His *wants,* and yours, may have to wait.

At times, giving children some of the things they want but don't need isn't a bad idea. Gifts to children can be a way of telling them that they are important and valued. However, they don't need candy before dinner, or to go out in the snow without putting on a coat. The things children want should not typically be given before their basic needs are met. The older your child gets, the better able he will be to wait for the things he wants, but he will only learn to do this if you start out faithfully providing the things he needs.

Like other parents, Mr. and Mrs. Green wanted to do the right thing or they would not have come to my office. But they had unintentionally let their own needs become the business of their two-year-old. Katie felt the tension and anger between the two adults on whom she depended most. Her parents had allowed her care to become part of their "ammunition" in their battles, leaving her distressed and insecure. Had Mr. and Mrs. Green not been willing to look at what they were doing and take measures to change it, I would have questioned their true commitment to successful parenting, but after giving it some thought, they realized that they had been upsetting Katie. They learned that children, even infants and toddlers, can sense when adults are angry all the time and become confused, frightened, insecure, or angry themselves.

The boundary between adult and child issues can get blurred in many different ways and create insecurity in a child. Hearing parents discuss their insecurities and fears shakes a young child's confidence. Watching parents argue must make a child feel the way you or I might feel if we thought the President was about to declare war. Hearing adults talk about the things their child does wrong must feel like hearing your boss tell someone what a rotten employee you are! Children and adults want confident, positive leaders, not ones who create doubts and insecurity. When they hear adults talk about their problems, raise their voices, or discuss problem behaviors, they are set up to feel insecure and threatened, and to react in ways others will notice.

Of course, parents sometimes disagree with each other. When they do, they may feel threatened or insecure themselves. Their immediate goal is to get their position across to the other person and stop feeling uncomfortable. Unfortunately, feeling threatened often causes people to lash out without considering how their words and behaviors will affect others, including their children. It is easy to snap at someone else when problems are difficult to tackle, but over time, not considering the feelings of others can build unhealthy patterns of interaction and teach children the wrong behaviors. Sometimes, when my clients lose objectivity and talk in front of their children about their disagreements, I ask them: "If you were a fly on the wall watching what you just did and hearing what you just said, what would you think about what happened?" For some, that is all it takes to help them see that they have burdened their children with their own needs.

Once the Greens stopped focusing on their own needs when Katie was around, Katie's problem behavior stopped. This didn't mean they left their conflicts unresolved or sacrificed their hope of a close and rewarding relationship with each other. Quite the opposite. After they learned to keep Katie out of their arguments, they were able to identify the important issues between them and develop solutions. Commitment to successful parenting is more than a *desire* to do the right thing; it is more than good *intention. Commitment is a promise that only rings true if resolution also brings action.*

An important element of commitment is separating your needs from those of your child. Use these questions to get an idea of how you are doing in this area:

How well are you meeting your own needs by:

◆ Having food, shelter, and weather-appropriate clothing

◆ Keeping yourself safe from harmful people, substances, etc.

◆ Developing adult relationships in which you feel valued and encouraged

(continued)

Do you show your personal needs or worries to your child in any of the following ways?

- I talk about my problems when he can hear me (on the phone or in person)

- I ignore him when he needs me

- I blame others in front of him

- I raise my voice at another adult in front of him

- I talk about him negatively in front of him

- I bottle up my frustrations until I yell at him or hurt him

- I use substances (alcohol, drugs) that impair my ability to care for him

You've Got to Get Up

Putting your child's needs before your own takes energy; so does not imposing your needs on your child, but these two basic activities lay the foundation for successful parenting. As when building the foundation of a house, paying extra attention to the way you build the foundation of your parenting is important if you want it to last. The effort you put into your early steps can make a big difference in the number of problems you face later on. If you build with care now, you will avoid developing patterns of interaction that require more energy down the road. If you don't, you will move further from your parenting goals. Successful parenting requires that you pay now or *pay more* later.

The Richardses were a couple who did not understand this concept. Mrs. Richards scheduled an appointment to discuss the behavior of their eighteen-month-old son, but Mr. Richards spoke first when they sat down in my office. "This was my wife's idea," he said. "I have a tough job, and when I get home I like peace and quiet. But Darren is into everything. He turns the knobs while I am watching television and pushes things off the coffee table. And he doesn't stop when I tell him, 'No.' I yell it a thousand times and he just keeps on going. I hope you can get him under control, because he is driving me crazy."

Clearly, other issues needed to be explored besides Darren's behavior, like how much time Mr. Richards thought he needed for himself, how he and his wife distributed household chores, and perhaps how their relationship was going. Parents always surprise me when they want me to "fix" their child without being involved. Sometimes the child has no real problem in the first place. They simply don't realize that they are the ones who have the greatest chance of changing the way their child is behaving. A therapist can't interact with a young child once or twice a week and make any appreciable difference in the way that child behaves in another setting. A therapist is only a resource who shows and tells parents the best way to respond to their child's behaviors. Parents spend more time than anyone else does with their child and, by applying appropriate techniques and teaching others who interact with their child, they are in the best position to make a difference. Good parenting takes effort, especially in the early years when children are most demanding and not able to understand or communicate well with words. The amount of energy it takes may seem over-whelming at first, but it gets easier over time if you do it right. *Your child is young for only a brief part of your life. Your effort during this time will make a big difference in the future.*

When I first met Mr. Richards, I wasn't sure he wanted to parent at all; he seemed to lack the commitment it would take. He was angry with Darren for interfering with his needs, mis-understood his child's ability to comply with commands, and wasn't prepared for the way babies and toddlers get into things. He didn't realize that children forget what they are told and are enticed by things they can't resist on their own. By sit-ting in his chair yelling "No, no, no," Mr. Richards only taught his child that adults repeat themselves a lot and turn red in the face. He couldn't teach his child appropriate behaviors unless he was willing to take action.

It turned out that Mr. Richards didn't realize the level of involvement it takes to raise a child; he was simply doing what he remembered his father doing. It took real effort for him to behave differently, but with coaching, he began to offer Darren some things he could do besides playing with the television, such as putting toys into a container, playing hide-and-seek, and bouncing him on his knee. In short, he began to pay attention to Darren instead of acting as though he were in the way. He even decided to set aside his interest in television whenever Darren was awake, to concentrate on interacting with him. Commitment means addressing your child's needs first, and it means *getting up* to do it.

How many times do you say or do something and sud-denly hear or see your parents in yourself? Sometimes we inten-tionally repeat what we learned—usually the things our parents did that helped us to feel good about ourselves. At other times, we simply don't know what else to do, and it is easy to fall back on the things we know. Sometimes, our early experiences serve as a deterrent: We recognize unhelpful patterns of interaction and tell ourselves we will do things differently. But even if you know that the things your parents did when you were a child were destructive, they may have provided such a strong model that you do them, too. It can take considerable effort to parent any other way. Deciding to be an effective parent requires that you think about what you are doing.

Whether the unhelpful behaviors and beliefs you bring from your childhood are minor and few, or major and many, you do not have to repeat them in your own parenting. By reading this book you have taken the important first step of increasing your parenting knowledge and enhancing your awareness of your own behavior. The second step is to use positive parenting over and over again. Technical skills take practice to learn to implement effectively. The third step is to monitor how things are going. Catch yourself whenever you do things differently and effectively, and congratulate yourself. *Parenting is a voluntary activity. You have active choices to make about the way you will do it.*

◆ List two things your parents or other significant adults did or said that helped develop your positive qualities as a child. List two that you think had a negative impact.

◆ During the next week, count how many times you act the same positive or negative ways toward your children—or toward others in front of your child.

Be Creative

At times you may think there are too many factors working against you to provide for your child's basic needs, let alone make him feel secure and wanted. You may be a single parent, finances may be a constant worry, or you may have to share your time, energy, and resources with several children at once. These are difficult situations. Providing for your child's needs can seem impossible when such stresses come into play, but things do not have to be perfect in order for you to be a good parent. Waiting for them to get that way can be a big mistake. *Effective parenting requires persistence, especially when things get complicated. It takes courage to look at the factors that cause you stress, and creativity to reduce them.*

Martha, a technical school student I had in a class years ago, was a great example of not giving up, and of using creativity to solve her problems. She was twenty years old when I met her; her son Kyle was two and a half. They lived in a trailer park three hundred miles from her extended family. Her husband had moved out when Kyle was born and offered nothing in the way of support. Although Martha faced financial problems because of their shattered relationship, she was determined to provide a healthy atmosphere for Kyle. She took a receptionist job at a motel while she finished her secretarial courses at school. Although she had limited finances and no family around to help with Kyle, she sounded positive about her situation.

"I knew I couldn't do it all myself," she said. "I looked around at my friends and thought maybe we could help each other. Carrie worked nights. Having her two children when they would be sleeping most of the time wouldn't take much effort on my part. She liked to cook, so we exchanged meals for childcare. Now on my way home, I pick up dinner at her house. It gives me more time to play with Kyle, and I'm not so grouchy trying to cook when he wants my attention. The food's better, too," she added with a smile.

Martha made other creative arrangements that helped reduce her stress. With one friend, she traded child-sitting every other Saturday so she could see a movie or go on a date. Another friend picked Kyle up from day care in exchange for Martha typing her school papers.

Being creative requires stepping back from your circumstances—taking a snapshot of your situation and studying it for better ways to do things. Martha couldn't have done it if she had panicked or decided it was impossible. She *wouldn't* have done it if she hadn't been committed to making things better for her son.

Martha and others like her showed me that there are many ways to be creative in parenting. Many aspects of the job can be adjusted to take off some of the stress, including your environment, your choice of childcare-givers, your schedule, and your use of community resources.

REARRANGE YOUR ENVIRONMENT

The first place to look for solutions that will save you time and energy is in your physical surroundings. It is funny that I should be saying this, because I remember thinking it was silly to have to chart the steps we took across the kitchen to bake a cake in high school home economics class. We counted trips to the refrigerator, the sink, and various cabinets. The teacher said it would save time and energy if we put the spoons near the bowls and kept the countertop by the sink cleared for sorting ingredients. Today, I see many similarities when it comes to arranging the environment for a child. If you leave the stairs open, you will need to retrieve your child to keep him from falling down them. If there are interesting objects in a room, your child will touch them. One of my friends crawled around on her hands and knees to see what might interest her if she were only two feet tall; she found matches, detergents, and treasured knick-knacks. Rearranging the environment can create less work. Build a shelf for your television if the knobs are too enticing, or remove the knobs entirely. Pack your books so tightly on the shelf that little hands can't get them out on their own. As one client put it, *"if it isn't for play, put it away."*

Many parents complain that their children would rather pull things out of closets and cabinets than play with their toys. Appropriate, non-toy objects around the house can provide hours of entertainment. In our house we locked the places that were off-limits and had a "treasure drawer" or cabinet in every room where our children could find things to play with. Into this we tossed toys from fast-food restaurants and birthday parties, and other objects that were not officially toys but were safe to play with (more than two inches in diameter with no moving parts or sharp edges). Occasionally we moved the junk from one treasure drawer to another just to keep the kids surprised by what they found there. They stayed interested in going back to check it out. We put canned goods, pan lids, and plastic containers in bottom cabinets and got used to them all being dragged out in an evening. They were easy to put back and safer than other things the children might have gotten into.

Baby and childcare equipment can also be a great help. An automatic swing can keep a fussy baby occupied while you make dinner; a music box can help your child sleep better. Mobiles and activity boxes, front slings and backpacks all make life easier for parents who need both hands free at times. These devices are great if you use them correctly, but they must not be overused. There is no substitute for basic human contact and interaction. Children need a stimulating environment that offers variety in what they see, hear, and touch. They will learn little about their surroundings from the confines of a playpen. If you use equipment to save energy, make sure that you spend a lot more time playing with or holding your child than he spends in this kind of confinement.

FIND OTHERS TO HELP

Martha, my creative student, gave several examples of ways to make satisfying, helpful arrangements with other people, but none of them happened without effort. She had to be willing to approach her friends, admit her needs, and propose a "deal." No doubt some of her friends declined her suggestions, but most of them were willing to help because Martha was persistent and skilled at negotiating. Communication is essential when you involve other people in your child's care. They need to know what you want them to do, and you must ask enough questions to know what they expect as well. Creating a satisfying arrangement requires several conversations rather than hoping for the best and waiting to see what happens. It is far better to negotiate up front than to have hard feelings later, especially when your child is involved.

You will no doubt think of other ways to involve those you trust in the care of your child; all it takes is thinking creatively about whom, and for what, to ask. When my daughter was not old enough to baby-sit, she was a "mother's helper" to several families, keeping their children occupied in their home. She gained valuable experience and the people who hired her got an inexpensive resource to watch their children while they took care of other tasks around their home.

When our children were young, my husband and I discovered that many other parents face the same stresses we do, working and trying to be good parents. We found others like us who had no family in town and could use some help. Our day-care center provided a wonderful opportunity to meet other parents and offer to share some childcare. All it took was identifying the children our children played with and talking to their parents or leaving them a note. We invited the parents to our house for a visit so we could talk while our children played, or we offered to bring their child home with our family for a few hours. Choosing carefully, we found several wonderful friends who were more than happy to have someone they could call on when they needed assistance, and who extended the same to us. These early exchanges of childcare resulted in satisfying relationships for us as well as our children that continue to enrich our lives today.

SCHEDULE AROUND YOUR PRIORITIES

Not everyone is good at keeping a schedule, and much of the time we resent even having one. The busier, and older, I get, the more helpful it is to write down what needs to get done. Sometimes I jot things down as they occur to me, even in the middle of the night; other times I list needed items according to the store they are at or in the order I need to get them done. The more I organize, the fewer what-was-it-I-needed-to-do thoughts nag at the back of my mind. I forget fewer items and take fewer steps to get things done. Of course, making a schedule doesn't mean I get everything done. Most people can't fit everything they would like to into a day; they have to be realistic about how much time it takes to do things. Setting up an unrealistic schedule creates pressure rather than reducing it. If you have more commitments to meet than time to get them done, you may need to decide which are most important and plan a specific time to do them.

In planning, parents often forget to set aside time for their own needs and wants, and this can be especially difficult when having a job leaves limited time with the children. Arranging ahead to go to a movie on Friday night can make the week easier to get through, and knowing that you and your spouse will have an hour to talk means you can hold some of your discussions until then. A night out once in a while can do wonders to revive a weary parent when the children are left with a caring and responsible sitter. Although you may have been promising yourself a night out, a shopping trip, or a chance to exercise, the only way it will happen is to pick a time to do it. Few relaxing things happen spontaneously when you are busy. *You must schedule ways to meet your needs so you are sure they happen.*

KNOW YOUR COMMUNITY

When my first daughter was born, she had a medical condition that caused her to cry all day and all night. We had no family in town, and my husband and I hadn't slept more than a few hours a night for several weeks. Finally we began exploring a way to get a good night's sleep and found an amazing variety of services in the phone book. We called numerous hospitals, respite centers, and childcare organizations and found that there were many people to listen and offer advice. We ended up hiring a very competent nursing student to stay in another part of our home with our baby for just one night so we could sleep. After that, we were much better able to cope with the crying. All it took was some creativity.

Try using the phone book whenever you have an unusual need. Call one agency, school, or business after another to see what they have to offer and how to access their services. If they don't provide the services you want, ask if they know anyone who does—and keep calling until you find someone with ideas. This approach can be especially helpful when your emotional resources are low. Some community service agencies offer a talk line for people who are depressed; others will keep a child overnight if a parent is overwhelmed. Many agencies offer counseling services on a sliding-fee scale, and parenting groups are available free or at a nominal cost in most communities. If you need help with something you can't do yourself, don't be afraid to pick up the phone and do some creative investigating.

When times get tough, creativity can be difficult to summon. To get your ideas flowing, consider the following questions:

◆ What can you do to your home to make caring for your child easier?
  –Can you move something out of your child's reach?
  –What non-toy objects are safe for your child to play with? Do you leave them in an accessible location such as a "treasure drawer" or cabinet?
  –Do you change the objects regularly enough to keep them interesting to your child?

◆ Do you regularly set a little time aside for yourself? Your spouse?

◆ What do you want to get done this week, and in what order?

◆ How can friends or acquaintances be helpful? What can you offer them in exchange for assistance with your situation?

◆ Who else might have faced a similar situation? How did they solve it?

Respect

Do Unto Others

AN ADOLESCENT CLIENT ONCE plopped down on the chair in my office and told me that all he wanted was "respect." He was a burly young man who dressed to look tough, and he had such an angry look on his face that anyone would have felt uncomfortable around him.

"What does respect mean, exactly?" I asked him.

He balled his hand into a fist and pounded it into his other hand. "They know I'm the king," he said. "I'm the Man. People respect me because they're afraid of me. They respect me because they know I could hurt them." He told me about several teenagers he had fought with.

Clearly, we had different definitions of the word *respect*. To him, it meant being feared. To me, it meant having admiration and trust. When I suggested my definition to him, he actually agreed with it. He said he wanted to be a good leader and have others do what he said, but he couldn't think of any way to get it without intimidation and weapons.

The memory of a grade school teacher came to my mind, a teacher I feared but didn't respect. The only thing I remember about him was the way he pulled down a boy's pants and swatted him with a paddle in front of the whole class. I don't remember what the child did to get hit, but it didn't seem very bad to me. None of the students could remember it later because we were too shocked and humiliated by the scene. That teacher must have thought we would learn from his behavior. I guess we did. We learned to despise and avoid him. He wanted our respect; instead he got fear and contempt.

I remember that the boy sat still the rest of the day, but his behavior seemed to get worse and worse over the next few weeks, until he finally left school. When teachers or parents use fear, pain, or humiliation to punish a child, the child may comply and act deferential, but emotional insecurity and resentment eventually show in his behavior.

Some people have gotten me to do things through fear and intimidation, but fortunately that hasn't happened much. Not surprisingly, the people who have inspired and motivated me most are the ones I respect, admire, and look up to, not the ones who threaten me. One of my teachers in middle school was strict and held to her rules, but I knew she wouldn't hurt me, and she never humiliated anyone. I did what she requested because I wanted to please her, and I didn't want the consequences she promised for failure. I respected her because she was consistent and fair, and I wanted her admiration in return. *Over time, even very young children learn how to react to the world by how others around them, particularly their parents, treat them.*

I witnessed a scene in a grocery store that is all too common. A small child in a cart squirmed and squealed, reaching toward the shelves to grab anything he could as his mother pushed him quickly through the aisles.

"Shut up," she said. "Stop your fussing." But the child kept whining and kicking his feet, picking things up out of the cart he was riding in. "Put that down," snapped the woman, snatching a banana from his hand. He screamed even louder. When he reached for the banana again, his mother struck his hand so loudly I could hear it. After a long breath, the toddler screamed in pain. I was floored by the woman's lack of respect for her child. Couldn't she just put the bananas further from his reach? Couldn't she give him her keys to play with while he rode around bored? Couldn't she see that she was teaching her child to respond to people with anger and aggression? He didn't respect her. She was someone to be feared, someone who could hurt him whenever she felt like it.

For some reason, grocery stores offer a particularly good opportunity to see parents who don't respect their children, and often, other adults. At another store, a child about three years old was wandering the parking lot as I was leaving. He walked across the traffic lane, looking as though he were searching for someone, and I hurried to catch up with him.

"Where are you going?" I asked. "Where is your mother or father?"

"My mom's shopping," he said. "I can't find her."

"Did she come out here or is she still in the store?"

"I don't know," he said, beginning to cry.

"Let's look inside." I offered my hand. "The store manager will call her name and she will come for you."

The boy took my hand, and we went back inside. Halfway across the store, I saw a stern-looking woman marching toward us, and the child left my grasp to run to her.

"Where have you been?" she said, bending over him, her eyes a few inches from his face. He tried to back away, but she held his chin.

"He was in the parking lot," I volunteered. "He thought you went out there."

She didn't look up. "I told you to stay with me," she scolded. "I ought to smack you right here. Just wait till you get home. You're gonna sit in your room all night."

"Oh, don't do that," I said helplessly. "He was confused. He's just a child."

The woman brushed past me, never looking me in the eye. I wanted to stop the boy, to tell him I understood, but I was helpless as I watched them leave the store. I don't know why she treated him that way. Maybe it made her feel better. Maybe she had grown up being treated the same way herself. I wished she had had respect for his feelings. He must have felt even more helpless than I did. She might have gotten him to do what she said by behaving like that, but I doubt it, not in the long run. He will grow to resent her and possibly intimidate others the same way because that's what she taught him. He may do what she says, but he isn't likely to truly respect her.

People who are raised this way often find it difficult to treat others, even their children, differently—the way they wish they had been treated by their own parents. It is hard for them to break the anger they feel for not being respected as children, and not to pass it on. Often they don't know other techniques they could use to teach their child how to behave, but even good techniques can be used without respect, accompanied by ridicule and berating comments. They won't make a child respect a parent. You wouldn't want your boss to hit you when you don't do things right. You wouldn't want her to tell you that you are stupid or punish you for something you didn't mean to do. *Always remember that you are teaching your child through your actions toward him, and that he also learns by your actions toward others, even when he is not involved in the interaction.* Use good techniques and show respectful behaviors even before he is able to repeat them or to understand their importance, and you won't need to intimidate him to get him to do what you want.

Children Are Not Little Adults

Many years ago, during an art appreciation class, my teacher showed paintings from the Renaissance period. He pointed out that the children in the paintings looked just like the adults. They were shorter, but they had the same proportions. No matter what their ages, they all looked as though they would walk, talk, and act like adults, were they actually alive. I think of those paintings sometimes when I see parents hurrying along, dragging a child who is virtually running to keep up. I think of them when I hear a parent telling his child to shut up or smacking his hand in a grocery store. And I think of them when a parent expects a one-year-old to sit quietly through a church service. *Children are not little adults.* They don't think, remember, or act the way adults do. To them, grocery store shelves, business papers from the office, and knick-knacks on the coffee table are just curious playthings lying ready to be explored. It takes time, growth, and experience to learn how to behave. *If you expect more of your child than he is capable of doing, you will frustrate yourself and him, and perhaps punish him unnecessarily.*

I once watched a man hammer shingles onto his roof while his three-year-old daughter played happily on their front lawn. He called once to his child, reminding her to stay in the yard, but as I watched from a distance, his attention waned, and his daughter inched closer and closer to the street. Fortunately, the street was not busy, because the girl spotted a little black dog on the other side and was off like a shot to play with it. Scrambling down the ladder to retrieve his child, the father screamed at her for disobeying him. Clearly he had expected his daughter to remember and follow his rules even when he wasn't available to remind her.

It takes frequent interaction and careful observation to really know what a child can understand and remember. If he is large for his age, he may look as though he can think like an older child. If he can talk and repeat rules, it may seem as though he should be able to remember and follow them even when you aren't looking. But children are impulsive, and their memories are short. When presented with something interesting and enticing, curiosity often wins out over self-control. This is not always misbehavior; it is exploration. Looking at behaviors this way can keep you from placing your child in a dangerous situation or punishing him for behaviors that are simply part of his learning process. Keeping a cool head about the antics of a person a fraction of your size can help preserve the precious relationship that came with your child as a baby.

Knowing what you can expect of your child requires that you understand his stage of development. At each stage he has different skills to learn, skills that can be thought of as his "job" at that point in his life. The best indicator of what a child can do is his age, because children develop certain skills at roughly the same time in their lives. But no two children are alike. They vary a lot with regard to the age at which they first learn each skill. Because children learn at different rates, some will be ahead of the others and some behind. Most will fall somewhere in the middle. Comparing your child to other children—or even the ages suggested here—can be a source of unnecessary concern. Unless your child is far behind, don't worry that there is a problem. If you are concerned, discuss your child's development with your physician or a child psychologist.

Although children acquire skills at slightly different ages, they acquire them in roughly the same order. In each area of development, whether physical, language, or social, children learn one skill before they learn the next, in a fairly well-established sequence. They crawl before walking and babble before talking. For the sake of simplicity, I have identified the skills that typically occur during a given age range and labeled each stage according to the skill that is most prominent at that time.

The following descriptions of child behaviors at various stages of development show how behaviors change over time. Understanding these changes is an essential part of respecting your child. This section is about what children typically *do* rather than how to *manage* their behaviors. It stresses understanding *why* they do the things they do, which is not always what it seems. *What to do* in response to these behaviors is covered later in the book.

BABIES (0–6 MONTHS)

The term "Baby" describes infants roughly between birth and age six months. During this time period, they are completely dependent on others for food, nourishment, protection, and transportation. At first, babies do nothing on purpose. Their behavior is primarily reflexive, meaning that they are preprogrammed to react to the environment in a certain way. The reflexes babies are born with are highly adaptive for them: If you brush a baby's cheek near the corner of his mouth, he turns toward your finger—a reflex that helps him find the nipple when he feeds. When he accidentally touches his open palm to an object, his fingers reflexively close around it, helping him to hang on to it and perhaps bring it to his mouth. He "jumps" or startles in response to loud sounds or being laid down too quickly. Until about four months, he has an "asymmetric tonic neck reflex," which causes him to reach out his arm in the direction his head is turned when he is lying on his back (a typical "fencer pose"). Perhaps this reflex helps him to look at the things his hand touches. For a month or two, his smiles are mostly a reflex too, but they get the people around

---

At 3 months, a Baby may GRAB YOUR HAIR OR CLOTHING.

But he can't STOP BY HIMSELF. This is simply REFLEXIVE, *not* SOMETHING HE IS DOING ON PURPOSE.

He is learning ABOUT THE OBJECTS HIS HAND CLOSES AROUND.

---

him to smile back, helping him to learn that his behaviors get a response and encouraging others to bond with him.

Despite having reflexes that cause him to respond involuntarily during the first few months, a Baby is not totally passive. He can tell the difference between your voice and the voices of strangers. He watches objects, first fixing his gaze on stationary ones and then tracking those that move slowly across his field of vision. He scans edges and corners, and, later, the insides of shapes. He sees colors and patterns and likes to look at faces. These skills help your Baby to learn about the environment and you.

By three or four months, a Baby's movements become more coordinated, and he can act more directly on his environment. He begins to notice that kicking his foot moves a mobile, or bumping an object makes it swing. Later, he reaches for objects, intentionally opening his hand to grasp them. At the same time that he learns that his movements affect the environment, a Baby becomes much more social, smiling in response to people who smile or talk to him. When someone plays peek-a-boo with him, he discovers that they respond to his actions. When he drops something from his tray out of sight, it is gone as far as he is concerned. He doesn't drop it to get others to pick it up—he doesn't have "object permanence" yet. At this stage, he simply notices what happens: Sometimes the object falls, and sometimes it reappears. This annoying game of "pick up" and interactive games like peek-a-boo are very important for the Baby to learn that he can affect his environment. Babies who are not played with or don't have objects and people to respond to them often show delays in their development.

Babies are particularly interested in objects that make noise or change visibly in some way when they are touched.

At 3 months, a Baby may KNOCK OR THROW THINGS FROM HIS TRAY.

But he can't PLAN AHEAD.

This is simply ACCIDENTAL, he is *not* TRYING TO GET YOU TO PICK THEM UP.

He is learning that HIS ACTIONS AFFECT THE ENVIRONMENT.

When a Baby gets hold of an object, he puts it in his mouth, not because he is being bad, but because he is programmed to learn this way. He is exploring and making connections in his brain, which form the foundation of later learning. He may even stick objects into your mouth, but it will be a few months before he can anticipate or predict your response. Right now, he is busy learning the connection between what he does and what happens next. With repeated experience, he will recognize your response as familiar. If you can keep in mind that this repetition is actually part of learning, you will find it less annoying. By being part of your Baby's repetitive play, you will teach him about the world.

At 4 months, a Baby may STICK THINGS INTO YOUR MOUTH.

But he can't PLAN TO HURT OR ANNOY YOU.

This is simply CURIOSITY AND PLAYFULNESS, *not* TRYING TO ANNOY YOU.

He is learning that HIS ACTIONS HAVE AN EFFECT ON YOU.

By the end of the Baby period, around six or seven months, your child will begin to understand that the world is separate from him. He will come to know that certain behaviors or events precede or occur with others. Thus, he may anticipate a bottle when you come into the room or being picked up when he is reached for. He knows that objects out of sight still exist, and can anticipate certain events, but he still can't *plan* to make these things happen intentionally. He cries when he is hurt or hungry or wet, and you come. Eventually, he will come to expect your response, but not during the Baby stage.

> At 6 months, a Baby may CRY WHEN HE IS HUNGRY.
>
> But he can't PLAN FOR YOU TO COME.
>
> This is simply PREPROGRAMMED,
> *not* PLANNING TO GET YOU TO FEED HIM.
>
> He is learning THAT YOU COMFORT HIM WHEN HE CRIES.

CRAWLERS (6–12 MONTHS)

Children generally begin crawling between six and twelve months of age, so children in this age group are called "Crawlers." Crawlers are significantly more skilled than Babies, both physically and mentally. On hands and knees, they are able to explore the world, which means they have an increased ability to get into things. A Crawler can travel from room to room finding objects to play with, including ones that aren't toys. His key to learning is to notice the effect of his behavior on the environment, and he explores the objects he finds in many different ways. He may drop, bang, or strike them. He may sit on them or put them in his clothing. He probably will put them in his mouth. By doing these things, the Crawler puts together several separate impressions of the objects he explores and forms an idea of what they are like. This experimentation is important to his learning process, but it can spell trouble if you haven't Crawler-proofed your house.

Crawlers experiment with people as though they were objects, pulling hair, putting fingers in eyes, or tugging at earrings and glasses. These behaviors are a natural part of learning about the environment, not something Crawlers do to be bad.

At 7 months, a Crawler may DUMP THINGS OVER.

But he can't INHIBIT HIS BEHAVIOR.

This is simply CURIOSITY AND EXPLORATION, *not* BEING NAUGHTY.

He is learning WHAT OBJECTS ARE LIKE AND WHAT THEY CAN DO.

Crawlers begin to use their emerging cognitive skills to connect their actions with the things that happen in their environment. If a Crawler accidentally bumps a table and makes a glass jingle, he can remember the connection, but only briefly. A moment later he may repeat the same movement in an attempt to re-create the response. Sometimes these experiments involve things that he shouldn't get into or that are dangerous. This is not defiance or wildness. He doesn't know the danger or how unhappy you will be about it—even if you have told him before. He can't inhibit an interesting behavior if the desire to know what will happen is strong enough. He is just doing his job of learning how he can affect the environment.

> At 7 months, a Crawler may BANG ON THINGS EVEN THOUGH YOU HAVE TOLD HIM NO.
>
> But he can't REMEMBER VERY LONG OR INHIBIT HIS BEHAVIOR.
>
> This is simply CURIOSITY AND EXCITEMENT, *not* SOMETHING HE CAN REMEMBER NOT TO DO.
>
> He is learning WHAT HAPPENS WHEN HE BEHAVES A CERTAIN WAY.

As the Crawler matures, he starts to figure out how he can affect his physical environment, and also you. Now, when he plays with your car keys, he observes what they (and you) do when they are dropped on the floor. When you put them back on his tray, he attempts to re-create the original scene by dropping them again. This annoying behavior shows that he is developing memory skills. He now has "object permanence." He knows, at least briefly, that those keys still exist even when he can't see them. He will cry or search for them, but not for very long. Your child needs you to encourage him in order to expand his memory and planning skills. The internal image he forms of an object when you repeatedly pick it up for him teaches him that it still exists and that he can anticipate your response. There is an important limit to what the Crawler understands about you, however. Remember that, in some ways, you, too, are an object. He has no capacity to understand your feelings if you get tired of the game or find it annoying. He is simply learning what happens when he drops the keys, and you are helping to teach him.

At 8 months, a Crawler may THROW THINGS TO GET YOU TO PICK THEM UP.

But he can't THINK ABOUT HOW HIS BEHAVIOR AFFECTS YOU.

This is simply EXPERIMENTATION, *not* AN ATTEMPT TO ANNOY YOU.

He is learning THAT HE CAN AFFECT PEOPLE IN HIS ENVIRONMENT.

As your Crawler's new skills progress, he will repeat sounds and actions he produces himself, like babbling, clapping, or smacking his lips—if you repeat them back to him. He may not repeat the sounds or actions you initiate, but he will repeat his own sounds if you do something he enjoys in response. Your Crawler might repeat his sound if you clap or bounce him up and down playfully each time he does it, but your response must happen very quickly after the behavior for him to make the connection between what he did and your reaction.

One consequence of your Crawler's growth in mental ability is the development of an internalized sense of the people he knows. As he becomes more able to remember and distinguish among people, he may develop "stranger anxiety" and be hesitant around people he doesn't know well. The arrival of a sitter may trigger hiding and crying as you try to escape for a brief evening out.

During this stage, the Crawler will probably become upset when you leave the room, as he develops a greater capacity to feel and express emotions, like fear and anger. He knows you still exist, but he can't think about you coming back, so he cries and follows you from one room to the next. This separation anxiety is strong evidence of the emergence of a new mental skill, not something about which to be alarmed or annoyed, even if it hurts your ears and arouses your parental guilt.

At 9 months, a Crawler may CLING TO YOU OR CRY WHEN YOU LEAVE.

But he can't THINK ABOUT YOUR EMOTIONS OR THAT YOU WILL RETURN.

This is simply SEPARATION ANXIETY, *not* BEING SPOILED.

He is learning TO REMEMBER AND DISTIN-GUISH AMONG PEOPLE.

Wanting to keep parents around often results in sleep problems during the Crawler stage, and it is easy to be trained by your Crawler to think you are her only means of comfort. All sorts of unhealthy bedtime behaviors can begin during this time, such as bringing her to bed with you, giving bottles in the middle of the night, and playing music to get her to sleep. But just as a playful bounce after she babbles can increase her babbling, your responses to these behaviors can encourage them as well. When your Crawler cries and you pick her up, she learns to anticipate your picking her up whenever she is crying. This is an important step in her memory development, but remember that she still does not have the planning skills to *intentionally* start crying in order to get you to pick her up. She will simply recognize the scene as familiar and your response eventually will teach her that there is a connection.

> At 9 months, a Crawler may ANTICIPATE YOUR PICKING HER UP WHEN SHE CRIES.
>
> But she can't PLAN A SEQUENCE OF EVENTS.
>
> This is simply RECOGNITION OF THE FAMILIAR, *not* CRYING TO GET YOU TO PICK HER UP.
>
> She is learning WHAT HAPPENS WHEN SHE CRIES.

In the Crawler stage, your baby will be able to differentiate between a friendly and an angry tone of voice and may cry when he senses that you are upset. However, even if you tell him "No" in an angry tone of voice, he may stop what he is doing only briefly. He will be unable to remember the connection between what he did and your reprimand and may do the same thing again very soon. A Crawler does not have the mental ability to store this kind of information or inhibit behavior, and the world is just too interesting to stop exploring. However, a Crawler can learn to be fearful and anxious. Slapping his hand will not increase his memory. This kind of punishment can be physically and emotionally harmful. It does nothing to teach him what is appropriate to do. He will need you to patiently show him, over and over, what he is allowed to do in order to learn how to behave.

At 10 months, a Crawler may STOP WHEN YOU SAY NO, THEN DO IT AGAIN.

But he can't REMEMBER VERY LONG.

This is simply LACK OF MEMORY AND INHI-BITION, *not* DISRESPECT.

He is learning WHAT OBJECTS DO, OVER AND OVER AGAIN.

WALKERS (12–24 MONTHS)

Learning to walk is a huge developmental step that typi-cally occurs between the ages of one and two years. This extremely active period is called the Walker stage. During this stage, your child will constantly be on the go, getting into things and loudly protesting any efforts to interfere with his activities. Because he may follow a simple request, like "No," or "Come here," it is easy to think he understands more than he does. He may react to your words, moods, or facial expres-sions, but he can't understand your feelings. He will repeat actions that produce changes in his environment, but he can't predict or think about whether you will be angry or happy about them. He can't make decisions or keep himself from doing something naughty all on his own. In fact, he may be so caught up in practicing new skills and affecting the environ-ment that he is completely unaware of your attempts to get him to stop what he is doing.

During this period, a Walker discovers that some objects go together, and he is curious about these connections: A toothbrush may be associated with toothpaste, a cup with a saucer, a spoon with a bowl. Although he may not understand the function of these objects, he is likely to try to put them together himself. If not well supervised, a Walker may feed the dog, stick a plug into the electrical outlet, or put toilet paper (lots of it) into the toilet. He may even put two unrelated objects together to see what interesting or exciting effect they create—like a hairbrush in the toilet or jelly on the floor. While you won't want to encourage some of these exploratory behaviors, they don't mean your Walker is a future delinquent.

At 12 months, a Walker may MAKE A MESS WITH THE THINGS IN YOUR HOUSE.

But he can't STOP HIS CURIOSITY.

This is simply EXPLORATION OF OBJECTS, *not* BEING NAUGHTY.

He is learning WHAT OBJECTS DO WHEN PUT TOGETHER.

Sometime during the middle of the Walker stage, your child will begin to understand when he is told not to do something. He may stop when you tell him, "Don't pull the cat's tail," but this type of reprimand needs to be given promptly, just as he begins to reach for the tail. If you tell him not to pull the cat's tail when you first go into the room, you may only call attention to the cat's tail as something interesting to explore. He will not remember the rule or even anticipate a reprimand when he reaches for it later. Each adventure, even if it has been done before, will be new again to him. He will learn best if you show him how to "pet the cat," rather than warning him not to pull its tail.

Because a Walker's memory is short during this stage, he

frequently repeats actions again and again, even those that result in bumps and bruises. Thus, he may round a corner at top speed, bumping the lamp each time he passes it. He does not have the memory to predict this outcome, nor the foresight to prevent it, even if he is warned ahead of time. As foolish as this may seem, it is part of learning and not something to be disgusted or angry about. He is not stupid; he is young and learning. Punishing him will not help. You will need to foresee the dangers your child is heading for and remove them, or stop him with a well-timed comment or reach. Your job is to keep him safe while he explores his skills and combines objects for growth and learning.

> Until about 18 months, a Walker may DO SOMETHING OVER AND OVER, EVEN IF IT HURTS.
>
> But he can't REMEMBER VERY LONG OR INHIBIT HIS BEHAVIOR.
>
> This is simply CURIOSITY AND EXCITEMENT, *not* SOMETHING HE CAN REMEMBER TO AVOID.
>
> He is learning WHAT HAPPENS WHEN HE BEHAVES THIS WAY.

Throughout the Walker stage, your child's mood at any given time is heavily influenced by internal cues like tiredness, hunger, or tummy aches and sets the stage for his response to the environment—and you. Thus, an activity your child once enjoyed may result in screaming or crying when you try it again. Be sensitive to his mood. If you react to a moody Walker the way you would a moody adult, you will only make the situation worse. Pay attention to what works for him, and remember that getting angry doesn't. His mood will change with attention to his physical needs or simply the passage of time.

TALKERS (24–36 MONTHS)

Many children use words before they enter the Talker stage, but many more are acquired and put together during this period. Words are mental symbols that are first used for things your child can see and later for objects not actually present. Words are tools for getting one's point across, and soon after a Talker discovers this he begins to assert himself by saying the word "No" over and over again—sometimes because his parents use it a lot. With the development of more language skills, a Talker's self-assertion comes out in phrases like "*I* do it," or "*my* book."

A Talker's ability to assert himself is not always rewarding to his parents. He usually wants things immediately and may be good at getting his parents to hand them over. Talkers want things done their way and may be outraged by any change. Cutting a Talker's toast into squares instead of triangles, buttering his beans, or opening a can of pears instead of fruit cocktail can meet with refusal to eat what you've prepared. One mother's toddler yelled for her to "fix it" when she cut the food he apparently wanted whole. Getting angry sets up an unnecessary power struggle; his behavior doesn't mean the same thing that it would if it came from a defiant adult. Talkers often say "No" to things they actually want to have; this is just another way they test the limits to see what will happen. If you act uninterested in whether he eats his food, the struggle may stop right there.

At 24 months, a Talker may REFUSE TO EAT WHAT YOU PREPARE.

But he can't THINK ABOUT SOCIAL ETIQUETTE OR HOW YOU FEEL.

This is simply NOT LIKING IT, NOT BEING HUNGRY, OR TESTING THE LIMITS, *not* LOOKING FOR A FIGHT.

He is EXPERIMENTING WITH EXERTING CONTROL.

Control of the environment, including parents, is very important to a child in the Talker stage. Just as he separated himself from other *things* in the world earlier in his development, a Talker must now develop a sense that he is a separate *person,* different from others. During this stage, he learns to use a variety of problem-solving skills to master the things and people in his environment. He may turn doorknobs, pull switches, or combine two unrelated objects to accomplish a goal, like squeezing toothpaste on the table to make a picture or mixing grass in the sugar bowl to make soup.

A Talker can walk better and faster than before, going both forward and backward, and he can jump, throw, run, and climb. When you combine these new physical skills with his new problem-solving and curiosity, some upsetting combinations can result. You may find him on your bed reaching for your light switch or pulling a chair over to the counter to explore whatever is within reach. Talkers also scribble with crayons, pens, and lipsticks—often not where they are supposed to—and they smear things that come in bottles or jars.

As annoying as these behaviors are, they build important skills. The Talker is learning to control his environment and make it work for him. Adults like to explore and make things work, too; they are just better at foreseeing the consequences and considering the impact of their behavior. A Talker is just beginning to discover objects and their properties. Supervision, not anger, is the answer.

> At 24 months, a Talker may CLIMB FROM A CHAIR ONTO THE COUNTER.
>
> But he can't STOP HIS CURIOSITY.
>
> This is simply LEARNING TO MAKE HIS ENVIRONMENT WORK FOR HIM, *not* JUST NAUGHTINESS.
>
> He is learning PROBLEM-SOLVING.

Somewhere in the Talker stage your child will begin to imitate the things he has seen you do or say in the past. This can be a real eye-opener. Hearing him scold his doll or tell it to shut up shows the power of parents' modeling on children's behavior. When a child imitates behaviors he has seen in the past, this delayed imitation marks a very important milestone in his intellectual development. Imitation should be considered as a possible reason whenever your child gets into mischief. He may not be trying to mess up your bed; he may simply be imitating you making it in the morning. He isn't trying to be bad; he is experimenting or looking for a reaction— hopefully a positive one—from you.

Talkers don't limit their attempts to master their environment to objects and their parents; they extend this behavior to

At 24 months, a Talker may CRUMPLE YOUR PAPERS LIKE HE HAS SEEN YOU DO.

But he can't KNOW THE DIFFERENCE BETWEEN IMPORTANT AND UNIMPORTANT PAPERS.

This is simply IMITATION OF YOUR BEHAVIORS or SHOWING CURIOSITY, *not* INTENTIONAL NAUGHTINESS.

He is learning HOW TO IMITATE YOU AFTER A DELAY.

their peers and siblings as well. Although a Talker may play near other children and imitate their play, he is not likely to play *with* them yet. If he sees a toy he wants—even if he already has one just like it—he may simply decide to grab it. He is too focused on himself to play interactively or share. Letting a Talker "work this out" with the other child is not the answer; biting and other forms of aggression often result from this kind of disagreement. Spanking or telling a Talker he is a bad boy is not a good idea either; he can easily be made to feel *he* is bad rather than learning *his behavior* is inappropriate. Remember that during this stage your Talker develops the ability to imitate you after you do something, even hours or days later, and this applies to language as well as behavior. Be aware that your child will repeat to himself the things you say about him, and say good things whenever you can. Don't let him build his self-concept on a negative foundation.

The Talker stage can be very trying for parents, but it is a positive transition stage from babyhood to childhood. Talkers love adult attention, which is obvious in the way they enjoy controlling it. In general, however, they want to please their parents, and parents have the advantage in shaping the things they do. Your approval of your child's behavior will make him proud of himself. Giving your attention is the best way to teach him the behaviors you want to see.

A Talker's major goal is to explore the way people *respond* to him; thus, he is likely to explore your attempts to discipline him, too. If you yell at him, he may actually repeat his misbehavior to see if you will do it again. He is not seeking your disapproval, just testing the connection between his behavior and your reaction. Although these difficult behaviors take patience and skill to manage, it helps to remember that they are part of your child's growing and learning. Your Talker is not malicious, nor is he *doing* anything *to* you. He is learning the earliest skills in predicting his effect on his environment and the people in it. Give him direction and guidance to channel his exploration in ways that encourage his learning while you enforce age-appropriate limits. He should not be expected spontaneously to stop misbehaviors, exploration, or even tantrums. The goal is to manage your child's behavior without having your responses become detrimental.

At 24 months, a Talker may THROW BIG TANTRUMS.

This may look like HE IS DOING THIS TO SPITE OR EMBARRASS YOU.

But he can't THINK ABOUT HOW YOU FEEL.

This is simply FRUSTRATION.

He is learning TO EXPRESS HIS EMOTIONS AND INFLUENCE PEOPLE.

THREES (36–48 MONTHS)

By the time your child is three, many of the difficult behaviors of the earlier stages will become more manageable. He will continue to explore and discover his environment, but now will frequently play with his toys in the way they were designed to be used. He will stay at tasks for a period of time, sometimes up to thirty minutes, and he will begin to follow simple rules in games, taking turns at times without being prompted. At this stage, these changes will make your child's behavior easier than in the past, but his memory will still be short. He will need your guidance and patience as he continues to experiment with objects, inappropriately at times if he is not supervised.

At 36 months, a Three may SQUEEZE ALL THE TOOTHPASTE OUT OF THE TUBE.

This may look like HE IS DOING THIS TO BE NAUGHTY.

But he can't THINK ABOUT WHEN TO STOP OR HOW MUCH TOOTHPASTE IS OKAY TO SQUEEZE OUT.

This is simply EXPLORATION AND EXPERIMENTATION.

He is learning WHAT WILL HAPPEN IF HE BEHAVES THIS WAY.

Threes become more capable and savvy as they experience their environment and the people in it. They enjoy new freedoms that come with their increasing skills. However, Threes are self-focused and goal-directed; they often want to do whatever they decide is important at the moment. A Three may expect the world to revolve around him—to wait for him and to wait *on* him. Gentle, consistent teaching of rules and consequences, over and over, will help him learn what the world is really like. He will need to learn that the world does not revolve around him, even though he is very important.

At 36 months, a Three may MAKE EVERYONE WAIT WHILE HE GATHERS THINGS HE DOESN'T NEED TO TAKE WITH HIM.

This may look like HE IS DOING THIS TO ANNOY OTHERS.

But he can't THINK ABOUT HOW SELFISH THIS BEHAVIOR IS.

This is simply THINKING ABOUT HIS OWN DESIRES.

He is learning HOW TO CONSIDER OTHERS' WISHES AND FEELINGS BY YOUR LIMIT-SETTING.

Assume Positive Motives

Understanding a little bit about child development is important in every interaction with your child. This notion hit me hard as I watched a father lift his two-year-old daughter into her car seat outside a family restaurant. He discovered that she had a spoon from the restaurant still clutched in her fist, and he began to yell. "What is this?" he bellowed, shaking the spoon at her. "You were stealing from the restaurant!" Just as I thought he might strike the girl, his wife pushed between the two of them, arguing that their daughter was too young to know better.

"I could be arrested for something like this," the father went on. "She can't just keep everything she sees."

"She wasn't trying to take it," said the woman. "She just forgot it was in her hand. Even if she wanted it, she couldn't know that was stealing." She grabbed her daughter and the spoon, and headed back into the restaurant while the man got into his car. This father was completely unaware of his child's developmental level. He expected too much of her and made the worst mistake of all: He took her actions personally. He believed that the normal, non-intentional behaviors of a two-year-old reflected negatively on him.

Another parent once told me that she came into the kitchen to find her twenty-two-month-old son striking her brand new cabinets with a soup ladle. "Bang-bang," he said, drawing back the ladle to take another swing.

"No!" she shouted, grabbing the ladle from his hand. She admitted that her first impulse was to scream as visions of her unpaid bills flew through her mind. But the boy hit the cabinet again, this time with his fist.

"Daddy bang-bang," he said. Suddenly, she remembered that her son had watched her husband hammer those very cabinets into place just days before. Her son was not trying to damage the cabinets or add stress to her life. He was simply imitating what he had seen his father do—and he probably thought she would be proud!

In a friend's backyard, I once watched a three-year-old girl proudly push her one-year-old sister on a swing made of molded plastic, the seat belt and front guard securely fastened into place. Harder and harder she pushed, looking to the adults for approval and praise. Just as we cautioned her to slow down, she gave one last push and flipped the seat completely over. Her sister hung upside down from the swing as the adults crossed the yard in a single leap. "No!" we shouted, wanting to yell at her for nearly dropping the child on her head, but she hadn't meant to do it. She had been trying to help, and this "turn of events" scared her, too. Fortunately, no harm was done, and her parents even composed themselves enough to thank her calmly for trying to help. They gently reminded her not to push so hard the next time. I was impressed with the way these parents avoided making their daughter feel like a bad person. She had been doing what three-year-olds do, wanting to help, trying to be "big." It was the adults' job to supervise the situation; if anyone was at fault, we were.

When your child does something you aren't pleased about, be careful not to assume that she meant to be naughty. It is far better to believe that she did it accidentally, at least at first, because there could be many possible explanations for her actions having to do with her developmental level. If you respond with anger and blame when she simply can't remember a rule or can't stop herself, you will shame, anger, or frighten her, and she won't learn the right things from the experience. If you respond instead by holding your temper and assuming she had a positive motive—that she was going about the business of being a child her age—your child will be better able to hear your explanation and understand your rules.

Assuming positive motives does not mean ignoring the rules of your household. Taking things from a restaurant is not acceptable; neither is banging on cabinets. But these rules need to be taught over time, as a child can understand them. That means calmly stopping inappropriate behavior and repeating the rule, over and over again, if need be. I watched a parent do this one day in my waiting room. When she came through the door with her two-year-old son, she told him, "Play nicely with the toys. No throwing." But two minutes later, the child picked up a block and tossed it across the room.

"You forgot, Joey," she said. "No throwing blocks."

"Oh," he said, dropping the one in his hand.

"That's okay," she said, "but if you throw them again, I will take them away."

Joey didn't throw another block the rest of their visit. This mother knew how to set consequences for his behavior without making him feel like a bad person for breaking a rule. She didn't change her rules or let her child get away with misbehavior, but she assumed he had a positive motive, and her calm method of teaching worked beautifully.

Unless it is absolutely clear and undeniable that a child is being intentionally harmful or destructive, it is best to give your child the benefit of the doubt. Give him the message that you believe his behavior was accidental. Attribute the best possible intentions to his action, then explain calmly what the consequences will be if it happens again.

When your child misbehaves, think to yourself:

◆ I will respond in a way that assumes positive motives.

◆ My response will guide him. I must show him how to treat another person.

◆ He probably didn't do it on purpose. Perhaps he didn't understand or remember the rule.

◆ He didn't do this to make me angry. What are some other explanations for his behavior?

◆ He was doing what a child at this stage of development would do.

◆ My response will help him to understand that the behavior is inappropriate, not that he is a bad boy.

◆ My discipline must help him learn, not punish or frighten him for what he has done.

Respect Temperament

Every child is different, right from the start. Some are very active and others are happy to sit and watch. Some love to be cuddled and others seem never to want to be held. Children vary in how active they are, how intensely they vocalize or cry, and how overstimulated they get by touch or noise. Some are placid and sleep a lot; others spend a lot of time fussing or crying for no clear reason. Some tend to withdraw from new experiences and others are bold and outgoing, never seeming fazed by a change in routine. According to researchers, many of these differences can be attributed to differences in temperament, a tendency toward a particular style of behavior. To a large extent, these factors affect how your child approaches and reacts to her environment.

Unfortunately, temperament sometimes has a negative effect on how parents respond to and feel about their children. Children who are particularly active, cranky, or sensitive to their environment can be very hard on parents. Recognizing your child's temperament can give you clues about how to approach her and what to expect from her in return, but awareness of temperament can also create problems. Labeling your child can be detrimental to her and to your relationship with her. *Early temperament does not predict later behavior in a well-defined way. It is a source of clues and possibilities, but not a determination of the limits of your child's ability to behave a certain way. It is not a fixed prediction about how she will handle every situation.* If she is "active" or "cranky," you may be tempted to allow her to get away with things she shouldn't, like not sitting in her car seat or eating meals with the family. If she is "sensitive to change," you may be tempted not to take her out to restaurants or to ever miss her naptime. It is good to be considerate of your child's comfort, but if you go to extremes to keep from upsetting her, you may lead her to expect special treatment and cause her adjustment to new situations or care-givers to be more difficult in the future.

Another danger in expecting your child to always have the same temperament is the possibility that you may adjust your parenting style too far to accommodate her moods. One parent insisted that her child could never delay her nap—even by a few minutes—because she was "sensitive to changes in her routine." She refused to take her child anywhere or let any-one baby-sit and got angry at her friends for calling at the wrong hour. Her adamant inflexibility made her and everyone else tiptoe around her child's schedule (and her room), and it created problems in her relationships and her life.

Another parent had a baby who woke and cried frequently, and she constantly told others how crabby he was. But she didn't set limits as he got older, and he was still doing it when he was three. She assumed this was temperament and that it couldn't be changed, and she never tried. Her son lived up to her expectations: He continued to need her attention during the night for years. As far as I could tell, she felt angry with him all through his childhood. If you find yourself labeling your child as Fussy, Picky, Naughty, and so on, be careful not to treat him as though that is all you can ever expect of him. He will sense what you think about it and live *down* to your expectations.

Respecting your child's temperament means knowing that it does not totally predict your child's personality or behaviors. Being sensitive to her moods without giving her a label will help you know how to approach her. If she is sensitive to noise and touch, you will keep others from over-stimulating her. If she is fussy and difficult to settle, you will want to give her the extra cuddling she needs. But respecting your child's tempera-ment also requires setting consistent limits and not being too rigid about the way you handle her moods.

◆ What characteristics does your child possess that you think are part of his temperament? When has he behaved differently?

◆ In what ways do you respect your child's temperament or adjust your schedule to accommodate it?

◆ Have you been able to avoid telling others—or him—that you wish he would behave differently?

Be Clear About What You Expect

Knowing what is reasonable to expect of your child is an essential part of respecting her as a person. Children do not automatically know what you want them to do and, because of their limited ability to think and remember, it sometimes takes a long time for them to figure it out. What if you sat in your office all day while your boss watched you work and every now and then, in the middle of your typing a memo or talking on the phone, she suddenly shouted, "No, no, no" at you? Worse yet, what if she burst out of her chair and slapped your hand for something you didn't know was wrong? You would be confused and perhaps frightened, but would you know how to behave? How would you figure out the alternative behaviors she wanted? How would you feel about yourself—or her? Everyone needs clear instructions and consistent, reasonable responses from others to help them learn their job. Anything less will lead to resentment and disrespect. *Being clear and consistent is an important part of respecting your child, and respect is an essential ingredient of successful parenting.*

There are several reasons your child might not know what he is supposed to be doing. Because he is young, he may not *understand* a rule even if you say it to him. Even an older child may lose track of what he is being asked to do (or not do) if the command is vague. "Don't write on the wall" is more clearly stated than, "Don't take those crayons over there or even think about using them on the wall." But even if a child hears a command and can repeat it, he may not be able to *remember* it later, and even if he remembers it, he may not be able to *inhibit* his behavior. If you punish your child unreasonably or change the rules on him, he will be even more confused and angry.

Don't Say:	Say:
"Quit it."	"Stop jumping on the bed."
"Stop fussing."	"Say it *this* way." (demonstrate)
"Get going."	"Put your coat on."
"Don't do that."	"Don't touch the vase."

A Crawler will not follow rules by himself. He will not remember to stay away from your knick-knacks or an enticing potted plant on his own. Even for a Walker, the best you can hope for is that he will stop playing with it when you tell him to stop. If you don't want to have to monitor objects in your home, put them away until your child is older. The worst thing you can do is to expect more of your child than he is able to comprehend. Then your reprimand will confuse and frighten him. *Know what is reasonable to expect of your child and make your response fit with his developmental level.*

The older your child gets, the more he will understand

the limits beyond which his behavior will be disciplined, but this understanding won't happen if you sometimes permit a behavior and other times do not. Children learn through repetition of words and experiences. Your child must hear your rules many different times and be disciplined consistently when he does not comply with them. You must be predictable if you are to teach him what is expected of him. Being inconsistent with your rules will confuse your child, and he will not take you seriously when you want him to comply. The fun of digging in the potted plant will win out over the possibility that there may be consequences. If you don't want to stick to your rules, don't draw the line. You must decide what is important; if it is not okay to play in the dirt, don't discipline him for it one day and allow it the next.

Consistency can be difficult when other people are involved in setting or enforcing rules. Children, especially young ones, learn rules and abide by them better if they are in effect everywhere they go, and grandparents, day-care personnel, and other significant caretakers often have differing expectations. However, children can learn to follow different rules in different settings if they are always the same within a given setting. It may take a while to figure out that Grandma allows juice in her living room and it is still not allowed in the living room at home, and the rule will have to be frequently repeated and gently enforced, but a child can learn the difference. A bigger problem exists when a child has parents whose rules are not consistent with each other or who change their own expectations a lot. This is much more difficult to figure out than having different rules at home and at Grandma's house. It takes consistent teaching and repeated experience for your child to learn to comply on his own. *If everyone responds to your child's behaviors the same way, he will learn the rules faster.*

Trustworthiness

How to Earn Trust Points

EVERY GOOD RELATIONSHIP depends on trust: We trust the people we care about to mean what they say, say what they mean, and do what they say. But can your child trust you? If you tell your child you will be at her soccer game and don't show up, she will be disappointed, but she will probably forget it over time. However, if you do it a lot, she may not believe you when you say you will be there, even if you mean it with all your heart. It won't take long before your child disregards your comments, and you as well, trying not to care whether you come to her games or not. Her resentment will come out as anger, defiance, or downright indifference. When your child is old enough to yell, pout, or intentionally ignore you because you have failed her trust, the problem will be obvious, but trust is important even when your child is too young to tell you she is disappointed. *The only way to earn your child's trust is to be predictable and reliable so your child knows what to expect from you. Your child will believe you and your relationship will withstand disappointments if you build up a considerable number of "trust points."*

BE CONSISTENT WITH DISCIPLINE

Having consistent expectations and follow-through are not only part of respecting a child, but parents earn trust points each time they follow through with what they say (or imply) they are going to do. You earn trust points if you stop your child from touching something when he reaches for it after you have said, "No, don't touch." This shows that the rules you set are important and that you will enforce them. If you tell your child he will have to sit in a chair if he hits people, you build trust points by putting him in the chair whenever he hits. Following through with your rules and threats of consequences for misbehavior is essential in building trust.

KEY PROMISES

Following through with consequences you have set is important in building trust, but the trust points you gain by keeping your promises of fun things like treats and privileges are equally important. When my daughter was a Talker, she fussed as we went into a store, wanting to play on the merry-go-round in front of the building. I told her she could ride it when we came out if she would help me by not whining for the things she saw. I didn't really expect her to remember the rule the whole time we were in the store; her memory simply wasn't that great yet. But each time she hinted that she might start whining for something, I called her attention to other things and reminded her that we needed to hurry so we could get to that merry-go-round.

Unfortunately, when we got outside, I forgot what I had promised. Her "Talker" memory was short, and she forgot, too, distracted by the rain that pelted our backs as I jogged across the parking lot with her in my arms. I strapped her into her car seat, climbed into the front, and started to back the car out of its parking space. Suddenly, I remembered the merry-go-round. We could have gotten all the way home before the same thing would have dawned on her, if she had remembered at all. I easily could have ignored my promise or told her we'd do it the next time, but I chose to make trust points.

Through clenched teeth, I said, "Oh, no!" as cheerfully as I could. "We forgot to ride the merry-go-round! You were so good not fussing in the store. Let's go!" I took her out of her car seat and trotted back across the lot so she could sit on the horse. By doing so, I taught her several things. One was that her behavior was noticed and was important to me; another was that there are consequences—in this case, good ones—for the way she behaves. Probably the most important lesson of all was that I was good for my word. I built trust points even though she didn't know how tired I was, how much I didn't want to get out of the car, or how much I had to do at home. *Parents get extra trust points for reminding their child of a promise everyone has forgotten.*

Why are trust points so important? Think ahead a few years to the night you put your child to bed, and she doesn't want to sleep because she's afraid there is a monster or a snake under her bed. Will you have enough trust points to convince her you are telling the truth when you say she is safe? Which parent is she going to believe—the one who changes the rules each time she does something wrong? The one who punishes her for fighting one day and allows it the next? The one who promises ice cream after dinner and then changes his mind or forgets? No. She will believe the parent who makes the rules clear, stops her each time she reaches for something she shouldn't have, tells her clearly when rough-play time is over, and remembers the merry-go-round. *There is a long-term payoff for being trustworthy.* That may be hard to remember when you're tired and it's raining, but you'll thank yourself later for making the extra effort.

> List five ways you earned trust points this week. Consider times when you:
>
> ◆ Did what you told your child you were going to do.
>
> ◆ Reminded your child about something you had planned but forgot.
>
> ◆ Stuck to a rule you made about her behavior.
>
> ◆ Followed through with a consequence you threatened.

Lying Will Get You Lies

There is something worse than changing rules or forgetting a promise, and that is out-and-out lying. I'll admit to turning more than one page at a time as I read a book to my toddler when she needed to get to sleep, but I don't think that qualified as a lie. Some are definitely more serious than others. As a child, I knew a parent who told his child that alligators would bite her if she got out of bed and not to go into the basement because there was a monster down there. My friend stayed in her bed because she was afraid to move, not because she respected his rule, and her father's lies made her nervous in many new situations she encountered. She was the most timid and fearful child I knew. I'm not saying it is wrong to joke with children; in fact it is good for them to learn that people sometimes kid around, that words and behaviors don't always agree. But this man was not joking, he was lying, and my friend was terrified. Frightening children is a cheap way to gain their compliance, and this tactic will haunt any parent who uses it, for years to come. Eventually, a child figures out that her parent can't be trusted, and the parent's words are not important or meaningful anymore. You wouldn't tell your employee there is an armed robber in the next room just to keep him at his desk. Don't scare your child this way.

I knew a parent whose behavior was like lying, but she didn't do it verbally. She would dangle one of her daughter's toys in the air to get her to grab for it, then play keep-away with her and not let her have it. She stopped only when her child got too frustrated to play anymore or did something aggressive like hit her, for which she would punish her. To me, this was downright mean behavior. Her actions told her daughter at first that she could have her toy, then she broke that unspoken promise. She thought she was teaching her child that she can't always have what she wants, but her child would have been much better off if she had been allowed to get the toy once in a while. *Children stay motivated to learn only when they succeed on occasion. They build self-esteem when they feel a sense of accomplishment, and learn to trust their parents when promises, verbal or implied, are carried out.* This mother could have helped her daughter feel competent, successful, and proud that she could take the toy away from someone so much bigger and stronger.

Good Technique

The last of the four ingredients necessary for successful parenting will be discussed in detail in Part III—Technique. Technique is the "how-to-manage-your-child's-behavior" part of parenting, and it cannot succeed without commitment, respect, and trust. Without large quantities of these essential ingredients, you will not implement techniques consistently or convincingly; your procedures will lack direction and have little purpose. However, if you are committed, respectful, and trustworthy, the techniques in this book will make sense, and you will use them at the right time. More importantly, you will have a clear purpose for using them.

Know Whom to Believe

Children are intricate and complex, and they don't come with instructions. As often as children's abilities and needs change, a training manual would require an upgrade every few days. No wonder parents rely on what they've heard from others, what their grandparents told them, and sometimes on what they learned from folktales. No wonder they read magazines in doctors' offices hoping to find a quick solution to problem behaviors. Unfortunately, much of what parents hear leads them to expect the worst from their parenting experience. Many parents fear the stages they have heard called things like "the Terrible Two's," but as in any new situation, they would feel more confident if they had some advance knowledge of that stage of development. Obtaining accurate information about what you can expect and practicing your response to a given situation will prepare you for what is ahead. *It is not reasonable to expect yourself to know how to manage your child's behavior without some preparation. No one would expect you to do a job without training or instruction.*

> Here are the conditions that are necessary for discipline techniques to work:
>
> ◆ Clear rationale—Know *why* you are using them
>
> ◆ Developmental appropriateness—Make them right for your child
>
> ◆ Persistence—Give them *time* to work

In order to be an effective parent, the techniques you choose should fit with your philosophy of parenting. Techniques can easily be done at the wrong time or for the wrong reason, so it is important never to lose sight that you are using them to *teach your child how to behave.* If your methods are shortsighted and used simply because they vent anger or stop a behavior for the moment, you will make the problem worse in the long term.

One mother I know heard an expert say to put her child in his room when he stuck his tongue out at her. She left him there for an entire day so she could "get some time-out from him." She figured that the longer he sat there, the more time he had to think about what he had done, but that isn't what he did; he trashed the room instead. She heard that she should take away privileges for misbehavior, so she told her child that he couldn't watch cartoons. She was angry that he didn't seem to care. Finally, she heard that she should make him do chores when he misbehaved, so she had him dust all the tables in the house—but he broke a lamp swinging his dust rag around, and she had to figure out another way to punish him. To top it all off, he stuck his tongue out at her again when she told him he couldn't have a snack!

This woman was looking for a quick fix. Not only did she misunderstand the techniques she was using, she also didn't consider whether her child's initial misbehavior was worth all the work and energy she was putting into punishing it. She didn't have a clear philosophy or set of goals for her parenting, and she didn't consider her child's developmental level. Since she didn't understand the purpose behind the techniques she was using, she could not know if they were practical in her situation or appropriate for her child. Even when discipline techniques are done appropriately, none of them work quickly, but she gave them all up, deciding that nothing works. To be an effective parent, you must understand why you use your discipline techniques and have reasonable expectations for their effectiveness.

◆ Think of a quick-fix technique that someone tried to get you to use. Why didn't you use it?

◆ Name a quick-fix technique you used with your child. What was the result? Why?

Discipline to Teach

What exactly is discipline? If I were to ask a lot of people this question, too many of them would tell me that it means to control behavior or to punish someone for something they did wrong. Unfortunately, few would tell me that the word "discipline" comes from the Latin word "discipulus," which means student. A student is someone who learns from the teachings of another person; thus, a disciplinarian is a teacher—one who guides a student, or a child, toward growth and knowledge. Appropriate discipline teaches children the skills they need to grow into healthy, confident, competent adults. By watching how their parents behave toward them, children learn how to treat other people. To be truly effective, discipline should produce long-term benefit, not just get children to stop what they are doing for the moment. *When a child misbehaves, discipline should help the child discover a more appropriate way of behaving the next time around.*

My husband tells of when he was four years old and tore all the leaves that he could reach off the small tree in his parents' backyard. This may not seem significant to someone who lives in a lush, green part of the country, but my husband grew up in the dry climate of Santa Fe, New Mexico, where trees must be watered and handled with care. His parents were understandably upset when he stripped the bottom branches of virtually all their foliage. They talked to him sternly and sat him on the step of his porch, then let him get up a few minutes later. Remorseful and sad, he asked for some tape and spent the next half-hour sticking as many leaves as he could back on the branches. His parents hadn't asked for this activity, and of course it did no good, but they watched him for a while, told him how much better the tree looked, and thanked him for doing his best to fix the problem.

The parents' reaction to this situation involved what I think is the very core of discipline: *Children should be treated as though they are basically good and helped to feel that they can fix whatever errors they make. Through some action of their own, they should be able to get back to square one with their parents.* Once a child has paid his dues through whatever consequence you have chosen, he must feel as though he is starting over without previous errors being held against him. He must feel that he is accepted again by you.

It is important to realize that although your discipline may stop your child's behavior for the moment, he may go right over and do the same thing again, depending on his age. This is almost guaranteed with Crawlers and Walkers, and it will happen frequently with older children as well. Choose a discipline method you can feel good about, one that shows trustworthiness and respect. If it doesn't feel right from those perspectives, even if it works in the short term, don't use it. Your child will learn by watching what you do. If you solve the current problem with impatience and force, he will learn that this is the way to solve problems. Take the extra effort to model the behaviors you want him to learn from the interaction. It will pay off in the long term.

There is a hot debate about whether to spank children or not, or even to slap a hand. Many people ask, "Why not?" They were raised that way, and they think they turned out okay. They don't want their child to get away with the things they weren't allowed to do and want them to know who's in charge. My answer to the question of spanking is, "Why do you need to?" The risks you run by doing it far outweigh the benefits. Spanking is the lazy way out and is rarely helpful anyway. All it teaches is that it is okay to hit someone else. Spanking may stop a child from whatever he is doing at a particular moment, but it won't make him remember the rule any better than saying "No" and removing him from the situation. The line between discipline and abuse is very fine. When you are angry, it is easy to hurt someone who is tiny. I have seen terrible cases of abuse by otherwise very good parents. Because they were in the habit of striking out when their child misbehaved, a frustrating incident triggered a response they were horribly sorry about later.

Use the Same Rules

Children learn best through consistency and repetition of rules, and eventually, you will want your rules to become part of your child's own thoughts so she makes good decisions when you are not around. Your child will not develop an independent moral code for many years; she will have only the rules you and other caregivers have taught until then. Of course, some people your child will encounter may have different views of child rearing than you do, whether they are relatives, family friends, baby-sitters, or childcare workers, and appropriate behaviors are learned best when children get the same messages in every setting they go into. One parent forbade her child to hit other people, but it was accepted at her sister's house. She wanted to make the two settings consistent for her child and finally decided to talk to her sister about it. She said, "I'm trying to teach Robbie not to hit by using time-out each time he does it. Would it be okay with you if we made the same rule and handled it the same way for all the kids?" Her sister agreed, and Robbie's behavior improved in both settings.

It may be difficult to change the opinion of those whose discipline techniques vary greatly from your parenting principles, and occasionally the only solution may be to limit your child's time with them. This can be troublesome with family members, and should happen only after a great deal of thought, but baby-sitters and childcare workers are another story. They are your employees. If they discipline your child in ways that don't fit with your parenting goals even after you explain your position, find other people to take care of your child. Find someone whose philosophy matches yours, even if their specific rules differ. Just because someone is in the child-care business does not mean they are necessarily doing the right thing for your child. Your child has a right to the best care possible.

Interview your child's sitter or childcare center. Ask the following questions:

◆ What are the rules in your house/childcare center?

◆ If a child were to touch your stereo, what would you do?

◆ How do you feel about spanking?

◆ Do you ever smack children's hands?

◆ Does a child have to take a nap? What if he isn't sleepy?

◆ What do you do if a child bites?

◆ Do you use time-out? How do you do it? Where do you put a child in time-out?

◆ What do you do when the phone rings?

◆ How many children will you take on?

◆ Can I drop in any time without calling?

◆ Can I have the names and phone numbers of your references?

PART III

Discipline Techniques

Your Reaction Counts

COMMITMENT, RESPECT, AND TRUST are three ingredients necessary for successful parenting; but having these ingredients alone doesn't mean that you will know what to do in a given situation, how to respond to your child's behavior. Responding to your child in a way that keeps your future goals in mind requires a fourth ingredient, knowledge of accurate and reasonable techniques. The remainder of this book discusses discipline techniques that, when applied in an atmosphere of commitment, respect, and trust, can be used to facilitate your long-term parenting goals.

As humans, we are affected by the way other people respond to us and by the results we achieve when we manipulate objects in our physical environment. If we get a positive response when we do something, we usually keep doing it, if we get a negative one, we often stop. It can be as simple as that. But we are also part of highly complex interactions with others in our environment: We react to their reactions. We learn to anticipate what they will do in response to our actions, we learn to influence them, and we become aware of their influence on us. This same kind of complexity is part of your interaction with your child.

Your child constantly gets responses to his behaviors from you and from his environment. Mashing his peas on his plate gets interesting results from both you and the peas. This section presents four basic types of responses people provide to each other and their children. The next section on Progressive Discipline discusses how some of these responses can be used to achieve your short and long-range parenting goals. Remember that successful parenting means being proud of the way you treat your child; it means not needing to hide from the neighbors because he has repeated your behavior with the kids down the block.

Behavioral psychologists think in terms of using responses to a behavior to guide or alter the behavior. Their goal, of course, is to encourage desirable behaviors and decrease undesirable ones. The four categories of responses they talk about—positive reinforcement, time-out, negative reinforcement, and punishment—are not new; they have been talked about for years. However, among parents, there is considerable confusion about their use. If you truly understand these four categories, you will see how they apply to all human behaviors, and you will be able to use them to encourage or alter your child's behavior. These concepts may help you understand or even change your spouse's or friends' behaviors! They apply whether you are old or young, male or female, rich or poor.

Know the Four Types of Responses

POSITIVE REINFORCEMENT

The most obvious way to *increase* a behavior is to reward or "reinforce" it when it occurs. "Positive reinforcement" simply means responding to a behavior in a positive way, one that increases the chance that it will be repeated. Among the most powerful reinforcers for most people are attention and approval from others. If you stood up and sang for a crowd of people, and they booed at you, you probably would never do it again. But if they showed some sign of approval, something that said they thought you were a good singer, like clapping or cheering, you'd be more inclined to sing again, particularly for them. Money might work, too, even if you didn't sing well. Money is a powerful reinforcer, as is obvious from the long hours people put in at their jobs, but the actual coins you put in your wallet are not reinforcing in themselves. If coins had no value in this country, it wouldn't take long before people would stop going to work to earn them. Money is reinforcing only because of the things a person can buy with it, like food, shelter, or entertainment.

Different things encourage different people, or even the same person at different times, depending on their circumstances. If you are lost in the woods and hungry, for example, you will not immediately be worried about your paycheck. You will work for food. If you can't find your way home, you may focus on finding shelter for the night rather than caring whether anyone likes you at the moment. Under ordinary circumstances, adults will work hardest for things like attention, approval, or money. However, money usually is not a useful reinforcer for children because they don't truly understand its value and don't stay motivated by the promise of the things it can buy. When not focused on needing food or sleep, children most often repeat behaviors that get them attention, approval, or fun things to do. Even a child's spontaneous activities can be used as reinforcers. Behaviors that a child would do often if given a choice—like watching television or playing outside—can be used to reward less likely behaviors such as doing homework or chores. All it takes is requiring that the child do the less likely behavior first. This is the same principle that is behind having to work before you get paid.

As you can see from the number of people who have hobbies such as sewing or painting, even making something interesting can be reinforcing. Adults like to build, create, and experiment, and children, too, will work for an interesting result. Seeing something happen because of what they do increases the chance that they will do it again. Even your infant can demonstrate this simple principle of positive reinforcement. Put a piece of yarn on her wrist and tie the other end to a mobile. (*Don't leave her alone with a length of yarn; there is a danger of strangulation*). Watch as your baby discovers that her movements make the mobile move. As she gets the connection, she will move it more frequently to see it happen again.

Positive reinforcement is by far the most powerful and important response a parent can give to a child. The importance of parental attention and approval in this regard cannot be overestimated. The chart on page 86 shows that positive reinforcement means giving a rewarding event or stimulus in response to a behavior. The arrow indicates that this increases the likelihood that the behavior will occur again.

TIME-OUT (EXTINCTION)

The next category of responses on the chart is "time-out." Since responding positively to a behavior is the most effective way to increase it, it makes sense that the most effective way to decrease it is to *remove* whatever is reinforcing it. This approach is called "time-out" because you respond by taking the person away from reinforcement, or taking the reinforcement from the person. It is sometimes also called "extinction" because you are working to get rid of or extinguish the behavior. Reinforcement and time-out work together to guide most of the behaviors people have. These two techniques can be used even with very young children to change their interactions with people and objects in their environment.

To many people, time-out means putting a child in a chair when he misbehaves, which, when used appropriately, is one example of time-out. Time-out can include anything that removes the child from a reinforcing situation or removes the reinforcer itself. Sitting in a chair stops most behaviors, at least temporarily, because the child is removed from the opportunity to repeat it. No matter how you do time-out, give your child the opportunity to try again to behave in the situation he was in when time-out occurred. If he misbehaves again, repeat the time-out. If he behaves appropriately let him know that you are pleased. Time-out must give a child a chance to *better his behavior.* Only then can the right behavior occur and be reinforced.

When time-out is used with a child, it must occur right after his misbehavior or he will quickly forget why he was put in the chair or why the toy was taken away. Staying too long in time-out gives him time to get embroiled in an argument or find something else to do that is reinforcing, thus watering down its effectiveness. The longer time-out takes to start, the less effective it is in teaching about inappropriate behavior.

Time-out reduces behavior by withdrawing whatever is reinforcing it. Whether you do time-out by withdrawing attention or by removing desired toys or activities such as watching television or playing with others, be sure to carry it out with commitment, respect, and trustworthiness. This process will be discussed more in the section on Progressive Discipline.

NEGATIVE REINFORCEMENT

Most people think that negative reinforcement means doing something negative to a person to get a behavior to stop; actually, that is *punishment,* which I will discuss in the next section. Negative reinforcement means *taking something negative away* in response to a behavior. Like positive reinforcement, negative reinforcement is a way to get a behavior to happen more frequently. Everyday examples of using negative reinforcement as discipline are hard to find, primarily because they

generally aren't ethical. They include things like hurting someone until he does what you want him to do. If you twisted
someone's arm, for example, and told him that clucking like a
chicken would get you to stop, he likely would cluck like a
chicken every time you hurt him. Removing a negative action
(like stopping twisting an arm) in response to someone's behavior (like clucking) is negative reinforcement. It increases the
likelihood that the person will do that behavior again.

Your alarm clock offers a less painful example of negative
reinforcement. You know how obnoxious it sounds in the
morning, and that the way to stop its noise is to reach your
arm up and hit the button on top. The noise stops because of
your button-hitting behavior, and this behavior is negatively
reinforced. You wouldn't do it if it didn't make the noise stop,
but because it works, you are likely to do it whenever you hear
your alarm clock buzz.

Ironically, the most frequent use of negative reinforcement
in parenting is the control of the parent's behavior by the child!
Let's say your child whines and cries whenever you say, "No,
you can't have a cookie right now," and you can't stand his crying so you give him a cookie. What will happen the next time
he wants a cookie? He will whine and cry for all he's worth
because he knows that will get him what he wants. In this situation, you and your child each altered the other's behavior in
a powerful way: You positively reinforced his whining, and he
negatively reinforced your cookie-giving! Your response
increased the chances that he will whine next time he wants
something. His quieting in response to being given the cookie
increased the chances that you will give him a cookie the next
time he wants one, particularly if he puts up a fuss for it. Be
careful not to let your child use negative reinforcement.

Don't use negative reinforcement to discipline your child
and don't let others use it, either. Tickling someone mercilessly

until they say "uncle" may increase the likelihood of the behavior (saying "uncle") occurring again, but it is not a nice way to get it to happen. *Negative reinforcement doesn't fit with the parenting principles of trustworthiness and respect and is not an appropriate technique to use in managing your child's behaviors.*

PUNISHMENT

Punishment is another type of response a parent can use to alter a child's behavior, but generally, it is as inappropriate to use as negative reinforcement. Punishment involves responding to a child's misbehavior by applying a negative, usually painful, stimulus. The most common example of punishment is spanking. (Removing toys or privileges is technically a form of time-out, not punishment.) Why is punishment not a desirable way for parents to manage their children's behavior? First of all, it hurts. If it doesn't hurt, it doesn't stop behavior, and hurting a child is cruel and inhumane. Second, it isn't necessary. Positive reinforcement and time-out offer effective and humane alternatives to physical punishment. Third, punishment doesn't teach new, appropriate behaviors; it merely teaches that Mom and Dad can be frightening people who hurt other people when they are angry or frustrated. This is not the way you want your child to treat other people. In fact, it is just the kind of behavior you may be punishing him for.

I saw a sad example of the downside of punishment in a hospital intensive care unit. A three-year-old boy had been severely beaten when his mother's physical punishment got out of hand. He looked at me with wide, innocent eyes and asked me why his mommy had hurt him, and I couldn't answer him. Perhaps she had just lost control. Perhaps she had been treated that way herself as a child. Maybe she didn't know the power of positive reinforcement and time-out. Your response to your child's misbehavior can show him how to behave and give him a chance to do things right; punishing him will only teach him to be aggressive toward others. *As a parent with purpose and principles, your discipline techniques should say, "This is not an acceptable way to behave, and it doesn't please me. But I like you and I forgive you. I will give you a chance to succeed in a different way."*

Here are several ways you can give your child a chance to "make things right" again with you:

◆ Allow him to help clean up a mess he has made, based on his ability.

◆ Give him an alternative, acceptable behavior to do, and reinforce it when he does it.

◆ Give him a second chance to "do it the right way."

◆ Offer him a way to "fix" what he has broken.

The chart below shows how each of the four types of responses to a behavior (positive reinforcement, time-out, negative reinforcement, and punishment) involve applying or withdrawing something positive or negative. The arrows indicate whether this response is likely to increase or decrease the behavior.

	Application	Withdrawal
Positive Stimulus (Rewarding Event)	POSITIVE REINFORCEMENT ↑	TIME-OUT (EXTINCTION) ↓
Negative Stimulus (Negative or Aversive Event)	PUNISHMENT ↓	NEGATIVE REINFORCEMENT ↑

Respond Immediately

We have talked about four responses that either increase or decrease the likelihood of someone, child or adult, repeating a behavior—positive reinforcement, time-out, negative reinforcement, and punishment. In order for these responses to change a person's behavior, they must take place very soon after the behavior occurs, otherwise their connection to the behavior may not be clear. "Wait till your father gets home" is not an effective response to a child's misbehavior. While the child waits, events will occur that actually are reinforcing, and the impact of the response will be lost. In the preschool years, if you wait more than even a few seconds to respond to a behavior, your child may not know, or may forget, which behavior is the focus of your response. You wouldn't sing again for a crowd that waits an hour to respond to your solo, and a baby will not move his arm to get a mobile to move if the mobile doesn't move immediately. *Your response to your child's behavior must happen quickly if she is to make the connection between what she did and how you responded. The younger the child, the more quickly this connection must occur.*

How soon a response should occur for it to be most effective	
Baby (0–6 months)	No delay
Crawler (6–12 months)	Momentary
Walker (12–24 months)	A few seconds
Talker (24–36 months)	15–30 seconds
Three (36–48 months)	A minute or two if he is told what will be happening.

Be Consistent

Your response to your child's behavior will be most effective if you do the same thing during each episode of the behavior. If you laugh one time when your child dumps the baby powder on the floor and sit him in a time-out chair the next time he dumps the powder, he will be confused about what is allowed. He may even forget which response he got last when the opportunity presents itself again. It is far easier for your child, and ultimately less work for you, if you can respond the same way each time he misbehaves.

Consistency is a goal to work toward, and no one is perfectly consistent all the time. It can be especially difficult for couples who have different views of their child's behavior or different levels of tolerance. If possible, make a list of misbehaviors you think should be addressed and discuss them away from your child. Decide how you will respond to each type of misbehavior or agree that one person will do the responding while the other does nothing at all. Arguing with each other about your parenting behaviors in front of your child is one of the worst things you can do to your credibility and effectiveness. Even though a young child will not understand the discussion, a long delay or a halfhearted intervention will not give her a clear, effective message. Hold your comments and discuss them in privacy. If you are unable to agree on your own, a counselor may be able to help you negotiate your differences and present a united parental approach. When you have agreed on a plan of action ahead of time, your child will feel more secure and have a better chance of learning what you want him to do.

Understanding the basic responses that influence human behavior—positive reinforcement, time-out, negative reinforcement, and punishment—is important in understanding why certain discipline techniques are effective and others are not. Focusing your efforts on positive reinforcement and time-out rather than negative reinforcement or punishment will not only help you teach your child, they will convey an attitude of respect and trust. The next section will help you apply these principles to your everyday management of your child's behaviors.

Progressive Discipline— From Least to Most Intrusive

NOW THAT YOU KNOW the basic principles of behavior management, let's put them to work in your child's life. In the world of a child under four, this takes skill and creativity because his understanding is limited. You can't tell a Baby to stay out of trouble or quit crying; he isn't going to comprehend, remember, or know to do what you say. Managing your child's behavior will depend on how you respond to what he says and does, and how you respond depends on the lesson you want to provide your child. "Progressive Discipline" helps you put your parenting philosophy and goals into practice by organizing your responses on a continuum. In the beginning, your response can (and should) be least intrusive to your child's activities, serving to guide his behavior rather than stop it; only if his misbehavior continues does your response need to move to actions that interfere with your child's freedom.

PROGRESSIVE DISCIPLINE IS BASED ON THREE BELIEFS:

1) The goal of discipline is to teach, not to punish.
2) Child behavior can be managed using positive reinforcement and time-out. Parenting does not need to involve negative reinforcement or punishment. These methods of responding

to children's behavior can be unkind or even abusive, and generally show children ways of behaving that adults don't want them to learn. They do not teach and can actually interfere with learning appropriate behaviors.

3) Children should not be interfered with or directed any more than is necessary. Therefore, discipline should start with reinforcement for appropriate behaviors and move to time-out only as the behavior warrants. Discipline that is overly harsh or intrusive has undesirable effects on the work a child must do to expand her knowledge and abilities. Minimizing your intrusiveness is part of respecting your child. It is part of helping your child reach her full potential.

Appropriate discipline techniques fall on a continuum from "less to more intrusive" with regard to how much they interfere with a child's activities. There are six steps in this continuum, which must be used carefully as part of an organized approach to parenting. In order for these steps to work, a child must live in a household where parental responses to behaviors are quick, predictable, consistent, and done with the child's interest at heart. Progressive Discipline is part of successful parenting and is vitally important to achieving your long-term parenting goals. Commitment, respect, and trustworthiness are the elements that help you decide when and how to intervene and motivate you to persist until your goals are accomplished. The following steps on the Progressive Discipline continuum will each be discussed in detail in the next section.

Create a Positive Environment

CHILDREN NEED ATTENTION

The first step on the Progressive Discipline continuum is to create a positive environment. From Babyhood on, the more

PROGRESSIVE DISCIPLINE CONTINUUM

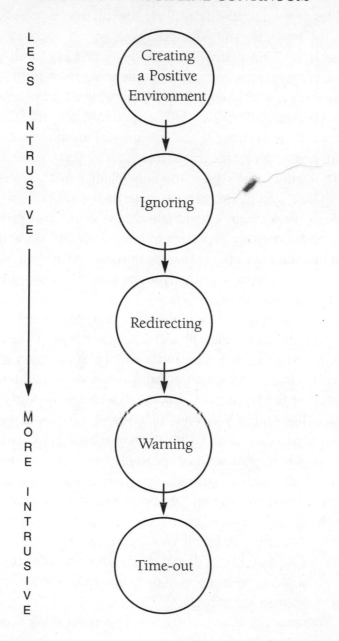

attention, interest, and respect you show for the skills your child is developing, the more likely she will work to please you and the smoother your discipline will go. Of course it isn't possible (or even desirable) to sit down and play with your child every minute, but it is a simple thing to attend to her, even when you are doing dishes or throwing a load of laundry into the dryer. Talk to her. Tell her you love her. Tell her you like what she is doing. Even though you are busy, take frequent breaks during the day to interact with your child. If you don't, it will be easy to slip into only telling her what to do or not to do: "Stop it, Heather. Get your hands out of there. Get back in the kitchen. Oh, Heather, how could you get into that?" It is extremely important to talk calmly and respectfully to your child most of the time, to appreciate what she is doing and give her the message that you are glad she is in your life, not that she is a bother to you.

Your attention is one of the most powerful reinforcers in your child's life: He likes it, and when he doesn't have it, he will seek to get it back. Sometimes your child will try negative behaviors to get your attention, but you can use your attention to increase the behaviors you want to see more of, and withhold it from those you want to decrease. *The more positive attention your child has in his life, the more noticed and effective the other steps in Progressive Discipline will be when you need them.* If you yell all the time, yelling at your child isn't going to get noticed. If you are calm and reasonable most of the time, simply changing the tone of your voice to a firm, but not booming, "No" will get heard. If you are constantly commenting about what your child is doing, in a conversational tone, simply withdrawing your attention or mildly changing your voice tone will have a big impact.

Parental attention is the most reinforcing thing that can happen in response to a child's behavior. Give her attention for

How to Play in a Nonintrusive Way

◆ Sit down on the floor with your child and watch him play with an object. Use a light, happy tone of voice and talk about what he or she is doing, just like a reporter. Don't intervene and don't interrogate. Just describe what is happening. "Oh, you have a truck. Yes, it makes noise, doesn't it? It's a big yellow truck. Now you're pushing it in a circle, ooh, up the couch. It's climbing higher and higher. Whoa, he fell off the cliff." Keep up this kind of monologue just to practice not intruding on your child's play, not giving directives when they aren't really necessary. Your child is learning about the world; you are simply making sense of it by putting it into descriptive words.

◆ In a pleasant, singsong voice, ask questions you don't really need an answer to: "I wonder what are you doing over there? Are you building a castle?"

◆ At dinner, play occasionally by telling your child what he is doing or eating. "You have three beans on your spoon" or "Oh. Good bite. Chew, chew, chew."

something she does, and you increase the chance that you will see that behavior again. Don't give it, and you decrease the likelihood of a recurrence. But don't be discouraged or think that your attention isn't important to your child if you don't see a change in your child's behavior right away. *Results don't always happen immediately, especially if your child is used to a response you have always had in the past. It can take weeks for a change in your response to be effective.*

One parent, Mr. Dillon, told me that he thought his child, Ben, misbehaved just to make him angry. His yelling and spanking only seemed to make things worse—he was sure Ben enjoyed it. There is only one reason I can think of that a child would like to be yelled at or spanked, and that is if he doesn't get much positive attention. Negative attention can be reinforcing if it is the only attention a person gets. From Ben's perspective, being yelled at or spanked was better than no attention at all. When he behaved appropriately, he didn't get a positive response; in fact, it wasn't clear that his father noticed at all. Whenever parents tell me that spanking hasn't worked, I suggest they take a serious look at the ways their child gets attention in their household. Often it is a case of too little positive attention for behaving appropriately. Mr. Dillon was too angry at first to notice Ben's good behaviors, but once he began telling him over and over when he liked what he was doing, Ben's behavior improved considerably. Eventually, Ben worked a lot harder for his father's positive attention than he did for negative attention.

Make the Positives Outweigh the Negatives

◆ Pick out two 30-minute blocks of time in the next few hours and count the number of times you say "No" to your child during each period. Write down the number of times you praise your child. Do you have at least twice as many praises as "no's"?

◆ For a whole day, make it a point to avoid saying "No" to your child. Give him appropriate things to do and praise him, instead.

CHILDREN NEED TOUCH

Touching is a natural thing to do with Babies because they are dependent on parents to move them from place to place, feed them, and rock them to sleep, but many parents forget that touching is an important part of providing a positive environment to their older children as well. Sometimes they stop rocking their child as soon as he walks or hand him a bottle as soon as he can hold it. As children become more independent, some parents think they should be able to soothe themselves, ask for what they want, and not need to be held, but this is only a little bit true. Touch is a form of security to a child; it soothes him, gives him sensory input, and teaches him things about the world. Holding your child in a position from which he can look into your eyes and study your face is vitally important to your Baby's attachment to you; it is an opportunity for socialization and comfort for many years. Even children who are too busy to cuddle in a parent's lap need the comfort of a backrub or a pat when they are tired and sleepy, or a hug when they are feeling extra cranky. Look for many opportunities to comfort your child through touch. Although children differ in how much and what kinds of touch they like, all children need touch.

Give a lot of attention through touch:

- ◆ Hug her
- ◆ Kiss him
- ◆ Rock him in your arms
- ◆ Bounce her on your knee
- ◆ Dance with him
- ◆ Rub or scratch his back
- ◆ Pat her on the shoulder
- ◆ Hold hands while you are walking

CHILDREN NEED PRAISE

Everyone needs to be told they are doing a good job once in a while: Praise is important to adults; children need it even more. Although any attention can be reinforcing, your *specific* comments about what you like about your child's behavior let him know exactly what he is getting attention for, so he is more likely to repeat the same behavior in the future. Giving specific praise is just one more way to increase the effectiveness of your reinforcement, and this type of reinforcement gets more powerful as your child develops the language skills to understand your words in more detail. Surprisingly, many parents have difficulty telling their children what they like about their behavior. One mother contended that her two-year-old never did anything she could reinforce. To hear her describe it, her son whined, fussed, or got into things every minute of the day. She was aggravated and annoyed, and by attending mostly to his inappropriate behaviors, she was unable to see any of the good things he did.

If you are always focused on the things your child does that annoy you, you will have trouble finding a time when he is behaving well, but there are literally thousands of opportunities each day to tell even the most unmanageable child that he is doing something right. If he is sitting at the table (even if he isn't eating as much or the way you would like), he is not running around the room. If he is quiet in his car seat, even very briefly, it is a good time to notice that he is sitting appropriately. Even if he isn't doing something perfectly, he may be making an effort to behave, to help you, or to master a challenging task. Say something descriptive of his behavior: "You are sitting so nicely" or his effort: "You're working hard to help me." *Do your very best to notice when he is being good and praise him, even if you are upset with other things he has done during the day.* Don't let those other experiences detract from your positive interactions with your child.

One set of parents told me that they were well aware of the times their child watched television and didn't fight with her brother, but they were leery of distracting her when things were going well. When their daughter was watching television, she wasn't crying, fussing, whining, or asking for anything. It was a low-demand situation and no energy was required compared to all the times they felt they had to yell at or correct their child. This mother even said she once crawled behind the couch when she had to cross the living room so her children wouldn't know she was around; she was afraid she would cause a pleasant situation to end. Actually, she had good reason to think so: When she finally said, "I like how you are sitting so nicely," her child got up and begged for a snack!

Calling attention to a behavior—especially if it is unusual for you to do so—is likely to signal your child that attention is available, and he probably will clamor for more. Over time, if attention is frequently available for good behavior, this will happen less often. It took considerable effort for these parents to praise their daughter's positive behaviors; they were worn down by her demands the rest of the time. However, as they decreased their yelling about her misbehaviors and began to praise her regularly, it began to pay off. Eventually, their daughter realized that attention was more available for being appropriate than for being inappropriate, and the basic tenor of their household became more positive.

"Leaving well enough alone" is reasonable some of the time, but it is a poor habit to get into. *Children need to know that you like what they are doing, and they need to hear precisely what it is that you like.* Otherwise, they are left guessing how to please you, and there may be little payoff for doing it. If you don't want to distract your child completely, try patting him on the back, hugging him, or just sitting down beside him— but be sure to tell him very soon what you liked about his behavior. With older children you can delay this kind of feed-back, but young ones need to hear from you on the spot.

Parents often forget to comment, or even notice, when their child is doing something appropriate or undemanding. Here are several suggestions to help remind you to comment on your child's (specific) good behavior:

◆ Put yellow sticky notes in all the places you look most frequently during the day: the kitchen cabinet, the mirror, your watch, the window—anywhere you are likely to notice them. When you do, turn around and look at what your child is doing. Is he or she playing without fussing? Smiling at you from the playpen? Pulling the cans out of the cabinet that you purposely let her get into? *Tell her* you like what she is doing. Talk to her. Smile at her. Let her know that what she is doing is okay with you.

◆ Be sure to seize the moment and praise your child before she starts to do something else. If she misbehaves after your comment, don't "take it back" or assume your praise isn't important to her. And don't attend to the mis-behavior more than you did the positive behavior. Just catch the next positive one, and praise her quickly. Catch her while she is still:

  -Sitting quietly at the dinner table.
  -Putting bites of food in her mouth.
  -Playing happily with the blocks.
  -Sitting in her car seat.
  -Staying in your lap.

(continued)

◆ In order to be specific about the behavior you are praising, try filling in the blank on any of these comments when you notice your child behaving appropriately:

-I like the way you are _____.
(Example: "chewing each bite.")

-Ooh, that is an excellent _____.
(Example: "castle you are building.")

-Good job _____.
(Example: "cleaning your plate.")

-You are such a good _____.
(Example: "builder.")

CHILDREN NEED OTHER KINDS OF ATTENTION

There are many ways to let your child know that he is doing well and remind him that you are watching. Think of as many ways as you can to get that message across—and do it as often as possible.

Use Other Kinds of Reinforcement

Here are other ways to let your child know you like what he or she is doing. Most of these will be more useful for Talkers and Threes. But you can start using them any time you think your child will understand them.

◆ A pat on the back   ◆ A smile
◆ A "thumbs-up" signal   ◆ A nod
◆ High-fives   ◆ A hug
◆ A bounce on the knee   ◆ A wave
◆ A wink

MAKE POSITIVE ATTENTION THE NORM

If you want positive attention to be typical in your household, it should not be limited to behaviors you are intentionally trying to increase. Give positive attention anytime your child is not misbehaving as a way of saying, "I like you, I respect you, and I have forgotten whatever misbehaviors you have done in the past." Some parents ask whether they should tell their child that he is being "good." This isn't necessarily harmful, but it isn't always helpful either. For one thing, you may miss an opportunity to teach your child exactly what you like about his behavior and to give him a better chance of repeating it in the future. Second, in your child's mind, the opposite of "good" is "bad." Is he bad when he isn't doing what he's doing right now? He may think so. Talking about qualities like good or bad instead of specific behavior runs the risk of making the child think you are judging *him* instead of his *behavior.* You can love him and not like that he stuck his hand in the toilet. You don't ever want him to think he is a bad person. It is better to say, "I like the way you are playing right now," or " good job finding a toy to play with" if you don't want him to think you are judging *him.*

USE THIRD PARTY COMMENTS

By the time your child reaches the Talker stage, he will understand much of what is said to him and about him. These skills can work to your advantage as you try to encourage appropriate behaviors, and letting him overhear positive things about himself can be extremely helpful in building his self-concept. Thus, the "third party comment" is a very effective form of reinforcement. Discussions between you, your spouse, or a friend that your child believes he is overhearing accidentally, like riding in the car or hearing you talk on the phone, can be extremely powerful, especially if you talk about the behavior he is doing right then. Try saying to your spouse something like, "Robbie is sitting nicely in his car seat. He's such a good traveler!" or "You should see what Robbie is doing right now. He's sharing his new toy with Jamie."

Although it is best to use the third party comment technique right when you see the behavior, it doesn't hurt to brag about it later as well. The goal is to give your child an image of himself as being *good* at things. Say to your spouse, "You should have seen how well Robbie rode in his car seat today! I was so proud of him!" or to a friend on the phone, "Yes, Robbie's here. He's playing really quietly with his toys and letting me talk to you!" This type of reinforcement should not take the place of directly telling Robbie that you like what he is doing; it is just another way to get your point across.

Third Party Comments

◆ Find three different situations in which you can discuss your child's *appropriate behaviors* with someone in your child's presence. Talk about his positive behaviors in the car, while you are walking with him holding his hand, or while you are talking to someone on the phone.

◆ List five positive things you can tell your spouse or friend your child did today. If you can't find a time when you can brag in front of your child, just tell him yourself and remind yourself to tell someone else when he is there later.

Whatever your child hears you say about him will affect how he thinks and feels about himself, so limit your third party comments to giving compliments. Hearing you speak negatively about him can seriously hurt your child's self-concept. At this age, he can't feel good about himself unless he gets information that says he is good. Talking a lot about his misbehaviors will tell him the opposite and give him no immediate opportunity to change your opinion of him by doing something right. The things he hears you say about him become the things he says about himself. The things he says about himself form the foundation of his self-concept. Deal with misbehaviors at the time they occur. Do not discuss them in front of him later.

USE OTHER REINFORCERS

Giving attention and praise are the most important ways parents can encourage their children to behave appropriately, but they can also use other things that children find reinforcing. The most basic reinforcers to all humans, of course, are food and water, but at a given moment your child could want a toy in the store almost as much! Naturally, you should never withhold food or water as a means of discipline, except possibly for a few moments when your child is throwing a tantrum; you don't want to directly reinforce that behavior. If your child is screaming, "Give me the milk," you might want to request that he ask for it nicely before you give it to him. That way, giving milk reinforces asking for it rather than screaming. For a child under two, wait for the inappropriate behavior to subside, but never deny a meal thinking that it will improve behavior.

Children often respond to basic requests if the promise of some treat is contingent on compliance. For example, "You may have a cookie after you put your truck on the shelf." It is not a good idea to frequently bribe children with treats to get them to do what you want, and using treats to get them to stop an inappropriate behavior is a sure way to reinforce the wrong behavior. However, offering a reward ahead of time is a legitimate way to encourage your child to behave appropriately. Just be sure to request something your child can do, and give the treat immediately after he does the behavior.

Some parents feel that offering food as a reward focuses too much attention and interest on food. Any behavior or activity that a child would prefer to be doing can be used as reinforcement for appropriate behavior. Tell your child, "We will start the movie when you are sitting quietly" or "I'll read you a story when you are in bed." An older child could be asked to help you feed the cat before you go for a walk, or to eat his sandwich before he plays in the yard.

Many parents praise their children for doing things like completing puzzles or drawing pictures. Researchers once thought that using rewards for behaviors showing curiosity and spontaneous learning might interfere with children wanting to do these behaviors on their own. More recent studies show that this is not the case. You cannot hurt a child by giving too much attention and reinforcement when she is doing something appropriate, even if it involves creativity and exploration. Even when your child does something wrong, like spilling the potted plant, you can build in ways to use reinforcement. Calmly have her help clean it up and *reinforce* her for cleaning up—no matter how disappointed you may be with the broken plant. This will be easier for you to do if you stick with fundamental parenting principles. Remember that assuming a positive motive is part of respecting your child and an essential part of successful parenting. It will keep you from harming your child's self-esteem by punishing something that was not misbehavior at all. Keep in mind that she must be able to get back to square one with you, to be okay in your book and know it. Using reinforcement helps to drive this message home.

Reinforcement in its many forms is vitally important for any of the more intrusive methods on the Progressive Discipline continuum to work. You cannot use time-out, for example, unless you have something positive (particularly attention) to remove from your child, or a way to remove him from it. The more positive and reinforcing your home environment, the more powerful anything that *isn't* positive will be when you need to use it. *You will teach your child appropriate behaviors and make your other interventions much more meaningful if you put most of your effort into making positive reinforcement a habit.*

Sometimes parents complain that they increase their use of positive reinforcement with their child for a day or a week, and it doesn't work. Usually these are frustrated parents who have children who are fairly unmanageable, and they have "tried everything" for at least awhile. Their children expect them to give up whatever approach they are taking, positive reinforcement included, so their behaviors don't change right away. They may even inadvertently "test it out" to see if the change is real. Many parents must persist for months before a general change is seen in their children's behavior. If they intermittently reinforce the *wrong* behaviors by attending to them or giving in to them, their change to a more positive approach can take a long time to get noticed.

A positive environment is essential to the success of Progressive Discipline techniques. Whenever your child does anything, your response helps determine whether the behavior will increase or decrease. In order for your child to know what you want to encourage or discourage, he must understand clearly which behavior you are responding to. Therefore, it is important that your response follow very soon after the behavior. Don't tell him three hours later over the dinner table that you liked the way he played today; tell him now, while it is happening, and he will more clearly understand the behavior you liked. Getting feedback immediately is even more important for younger children, children with attention difficulties, and children with developmental delays.

A POSITIVE ENVIRONMENT means...

◆ Holding and touching her

◆ Playing with her

◆ Following and commenting on her behaviors

◆ Noticing and praising her good behavior

◆ Assuming positive motives

Below is an example of using a positive environment to encourage a child's behavior. This example will be used in each of the six steps of Progressive Discipline to show how your response should proceed as a child's behavior requires more intrusive intervention.

	Walkers	*Talkers and Threes*
Child eats appropriately.		
Create a Positive Environment	Parents comment about how nicely he is eating, and say things like, "Is that sandwich good?"	Parents give specific comments about how he is sitting or using utensils. They say things like, "You're eating a good supper tonight."

Ignore Misbehavior

The next step in progressive discipline involves being careful not to do anything in response to a child's *misbehavior* that might be seen as attention. In households where positive attention is prevalent, withdrawing attention is likely to be noticed and to decrease any behavior it follows. I remember a time when my husband and I were talking at the dinner table and did not speak to our eighteen-month-old for several minutes. When we turned to look at her, she became silly and displayed the contents of her mouth to us. We looked away and continued our conversation as though we hadn't noticed, and tried not to laugh. After a few seconds, we turned to our daughter again, and she was smiling but had closed her mouth.

At eighteen months this behavior was cute. But although it was not terribly naughty, it was not the way we wanted our daughter to get our attention. We knew she was looking for a reaction, and we didn't want to encourage it. Had we laughed, she would have realized we thought it was cute and continued her antics. Had we overreacted by becoming angry, we still would have given her the message that this behavior could have a real effect on us. Instead, the least intrusive approach was simply to ignore the behavior, as if it hadn't happened. Such relatively minor incidents are perfect opportunities to practice giving attention to the behaviors you want to increase and withholding it from behaviors you want to decrease. However, these responses are effective only if the child can tell the difference.

When you decide to ignore misbehavior, it is important to ignore it completely. If the behavior was done to gain your attention, the eventual result will be a decrease in that behavior. However, *when a behavior is first ignored, it may become more frequent or stronger before it starts to decrease.* This is particularly true if the behavior has received a lot of attention in the past, or if you have occasionally been unsuccessful at completely ignoring it and have given a hint that it affected you. Weeks can go by with you not responding to a behavior before the behavior decreases in frequency, which is why ignoring should not be used for dangerous or hurtful behaviors, or those for which you have too little tolerance.

Ignoring is a very simple, effective discipline tool, but what if your child is used to getting your response? To take an extreme example, what if she learns to pull down your adult sister's skirt, and everyone at your family get-together thinks this is funny? Suppose the next day she pulls on someone else's skirt and gets a lot of attention. If you decide this behavior isn't funny anymore, you might instruct everyone to ignore your child when she does it, to give her other things to do instead, and to reinforce anything else she does that is appropriate. This change in attention should stop the behavior. But what happens at the next family gathering when she pulls on Aunt Mary's skirt again, and no one laughs? Does she quit right away? No! She is used to the reinforcement. She thinks, *Where is my audience? Where is my laugh? Something is wrong!* When your child's usual behavior doesn't get her the attention she is used to, she is likely to do what behavioral psychologists call "an extinction burst." She will probably pull on Aunt Mary's skirt again, even more obviously, or try the behavior harder, faster, or more dramatically to see if she can get the reaction she expected.

Think about your own process of learning that something that once got you a positive response is no longer going to be reinforcing—situations in which you had an extinction burst. At work there is a pop machine that I put money into every afternoon. Each time I put my coins in, pop comes out. But one day I put in my quarters and nothing happened. *It's always worked before,* I thought. *And pop would taste so good!* I had an extinction burst before I finally gave up: I jiggled the handle, tried to shake the machine, and finally put more quarters in it! It kept them too; no pop. Realizing what was happening, I stopped after that—a relatively short extinction burst for most behaviors—but the point is I didn't just walk away after I first pushed the button and nothing happened. I had to find out for myself that the machine wasn't going to respond. A behavior that is well practiced and deeply ingrained can take a long time to extinguish. *You can expect it to get worse before it gets better when it is ignored.*

Behavior that gets occasionally reinforced, like gambling, can take even longer to extinguish. Someone who puts dollars into a slot machine all night long may think about quitting, but each time a few extra coins come out, she is reminded that more reinforcement is possible if she just persists with her behavior. This type of intermittent reinforcement makes some behaviors very durable and hard to change. Remember this when you think, "It won't hurt to give in just this once." If you give in to, laugh, or otherwise reinforce your child's inappropriate behavior, even occasionally, you may have a terrible time getting rid of the behavior later.

There are many examples of using positive reinforcement and ignoring to gradually help a child understand what you want him or her to do. When my Crawler was getting used to being in a pool, we tried to teach her to kick her feet. First we pushed her around in the water just to get her to laugh. She loved the feeling of moving through the water. Then we stood still with her, moved her feet, and told her to "kick, kick, kick." When she kicked her feet herself, we moved her forward in the water. When she stopped, we stopped moving her. We'd say "kick, kick, kick," she'd kick, and we'd move her forward again. This is a small example of using a reinforcing behavior to increase a desired behavior, and withholding reinforcement when the behavior is absent.

Another such example occurred when I tried to get our daughter to keep her mouth open long enough to let me brush her teeth. She loved to be sung to, so I'd start a song just as she opened her mouth to let the toothbrush in. I'd keep singing as I brushed, unless she clamped down on the toothbrush or moved away; then I'd stop singing. As soon as she opened her mouth, I'd sing more of the song. Using reinforcement and ignoring this way was an easy way to train my daughter to keep her mouth open.. The only way she could get me to sing was to comply with what I wanted her to do.

	Walkers	Talkers and Threes
Child eats appropriately.		
Create a Positive Environment	Parents comment about how nicely he is eating, and say things like, "Is that sandwich good?"	Parents give specific comments about how he is sitting or using utensils. They say things like, "You're eating a good supper tonight."
Child waves sandwich in the air.		
Ignore Misbehavior	Parents keep talking to each other without acknowledging the behavior.	Parents keep talking to each other without acknowledging the behavior.

Distract or Redirect from Misbehavior

Children sometimes do things intentionally to irritate their parents, but more often they do things they find interesting, and they just happen to annoy their parents. Many, many of these annoying behaviors are worth ignoring, but sometimes it is not attention that is reinforcing or maintaining the behavior. A child who is experimenting with his environment may find the activity reinforcing enough to keep the behavior going. In this case, ignoring the behavior might not work; it could take a long time before your child notices you are not attending and does something appropriate that you can reinforce. In this case, *it may help to distract your child from his misbehavior by calling his attention to something else or giving him an alternative behavior to do.* Distracting him can cause him to forget his activity and give him a different idea of what to do at the moment; directing him to do a specific behavior can help him know exactly what else to do. Both distracting and redirecting help your child find something to do for which you will give him attention. Be sure to praise him when he does it.

When my daughter was fourteen months old, she fidgeted all the time at the dinner table. We continually had to remind her to stay in her seat, eat, and not to draw attention to herself by playing with her food. When she waved her sandwich in the air, all it took was ignoring that particular behavior and redirecting her by telling her to do something else like, "Look for Mickey Mouse on your plate." When she reached and whined for a cereal box she wasn't supposed to have, all it took was asking her if she had raisins in her cereal to get her attention back to eating. Then it was easy to say in a happy tone of voice, "Yes, you do have raisins. I can see them in there!" which reinforced her interest in her food.

The most efficient redirecting command you can use is one that suggests a behavior that can't be done at the same time as the current misbehavior. For example, if your child is about to take a toy from another child and you say, "Ricky, will you please bring me my purse" or "Come look at this book with me," he will not be able to do the misbehavior if he complies with your request. You will make it impossible for him take a toy away from the other child because he will be going in a different direction. When he follows your direction or does some other appropriate behavior, be sure to reinforce it with your praise and attention.

A nineteen-month-old boy in my waiting room brought his mother one tissue after another from the box on the table, and I heard her ask him if he could lay them out on the floor to make stepping-stones to walk on. When he turned his attention to the task of laying out stepping-stones, she swiftly

	Walkers	*Talkers and Threes*
Child eats appropriately.		
Create a Positive Environment	Parents comment about how nicely he is eating, and say things like, "Is that sandwich good?"	Parents give specific comments about how he is sitting or using utensils. They say things like, "You're eating a good supper tonight."
Child waves sandwich in the air.		
Ignore Misbehavior	Parents keep talking to each other without acknowledging the behavior.	Parents keep talking to each other without acknowledging the behavior.
Child waves sandwich in the air more vigorously.		
Distract or Redirect	Parents comment on something having to do with the sandwich in his hand, like, "Do you have cheese in that sandwich?"	Parents comment on something to cause him to look at the sandwich in his hand, like, "Did I put ketchup on your sandwich?"

put the tissue box up on the reception window where he couldn't reach it, and he forgot about it for quite a while. When he reached and whined for the box later, she took out some crayons and a paper from her purse and started drawing. "Look at this face, Johnny. It's smiling at me." When he came over to look, she gave him a crayon—and the stepping-stones were long forgotten. This was an astute mother. She was skilled at ignoring what she didn't need to reprimand (after all, his interest in the tissues was only curiosity and they were right there for him to play with). She simply ignored his inappropriate behaviors and found others to attract him to. As soon as he was playing appropriately, she commented on his good job. This is not easy for everyone to do, but it works with children of all ages, whether they are whining for a toy or fighting with their siblings.

Tell to Stop and Redirect

DISTRACTING FROM MISBEHAVIOR is an effective step in the Progressive Discipline continuum and can stop misbehavior without more intrusive discipline, but sometimes behaviors can't be ignored or simply redirected, like when your child heads for the wall with her markers or does something that could harm someone else. Under these circumstances, she will need to be stopped before the misbehavior occurs. You can't take the chance that she will hear and comply with your redirection if she is about to hit her sister. Slapping or spanking her is unnecessary and ineffective; it doesn't teach her anything except to fear you. Remember that punishment will suppress behavior only if it is intense, and pain will not help complex learning. The behavior most likely to be generated by using physical punishment is anxiety. To stop your child from what she is doing without physical punishment, tell her "No" sharply and/or gently restrain her by placing your hands on her shoulders or moving her away, then suggest an alternative behavior.

Giving a clear directive about what you want your child to stop doing, followed by a suggestion of an acceptable behavior, is the next least intrusive step in the Progressive Discipline process. As long as you give your child an alternative, you aren't being negative, you are teaching limits and acceptable behaviors. Eventually, he will learn to find something else to do when he is told no; you are simply helping him learn this skill. Be clear about both commands: what *not* to do and what *to* do. Pointing to a house while you are driving along may distract your child from trying to climb out of his car seat, but he may not know what you want him to stop doing. Instead, make your request specific by firmly saying: "Stop climbing. Sit in your seat." Then change your voice tone and add, "Hey, look at that red house." At times you may be able simply to redirect your child's behavior without telling him to stop what he is doing. This is worth a try initially since it avoids calling attention to the misbehavior, but it may not be enough, and he will need to be told to stop. Very young children cannot understand a verbal request at all, and you will need to rely on distraction techniques.

A young child, especially a Walker or Talker, often can't stop himself the next time the opportunity for an interesting, but inappropriate, behavior occurs. He may not remember the rule, inhibit his behavior, or change what he wants to do. Teach him what is okay to do by saying firmly, "No, don't put the brush in the sink." Then quickly change your tone to a calm, lilting one: "Here, brush your hair with it." This teaches your child what not to do as well as something acceptable he can do with the object he has already chosen to explore (the brush in his hand). Think like a child and come up with a fun alternative activity. If possible, give him something to do that is similar to what he shouldn't be doing, but is allowed. If he

	Walkers	Talkers and Threes
Child eats appropriately.		
Create a Positive Environment	Parents comment about how nicely he is eating, and say things like, "Is that sandwich good?"	Parents give specific comments about how he is sitting or using utensils. They say things like, "You're eating a good supper tonight."
Child waves sandwich in the air.		
Ignore Misbehavior	Parents keep talking to each other without acknowledging the behavior.	Parents keep talking to each other without acknowledging the behavior.
Child waves sandwich in the air more vigorously.		
Distract or Redirect	Parents comment on something having to do with the sandwich in his hand, like, "Do you have cheese in that sandwich?"	Parents comment on something to cause him to look at the sandwich in his hand, like, "Did I put ketchup on your sandwich?"
Child examines sandwich, then waves it around as if to throw it.		
Tell to Stop and Redirect	Parents tell him what *not* to do: "Don't throw," and what *to* do: "Put it on your plate and put some ketchup on it."	Parents tell him what *not* to do: "Don't throw," and what *to* do: "Cut it in squares and see how it looks."

is heading for the wall with the markers, stop him with a firm "No, Alex," then describe the behavior that is wrong: "Don't write on the wall." Quickly switch to a lighter, singsong voice and say, "Here, I have some special paper you can use to write on." You will have stopped the inappropriate behavior and labeled it for him, using your voice tone to support your words, and you will have given him something appropriate to do with the object in his hand. *Giving an appropriate alternative to misbehavior is an excellent way to teach your child how to behave. It will help him learn to find something else to do when he can't do what he wants and make him a better problem-solver in the long run.*

Warn of Consequences

After you have said not to do something and you have provided alternatives that have not been effective, it is time to warn of what you will do if your child doesn't stop. There are two exceptions to this: 1) When you don't have time to give a warning (as with a child who is hitting her sibling), and 2) If she is too young to understand what you say. Clearly, if a child of any age is hurting someone or might hurt herself, you can't afford to request several times that she stop. However, in most other situations, you can teach your child that you are serious and give her a chance to correct her behavior by telling her what your next move will be. Giving a warning is especially important if you are teaching a new skill or if you have failed to notice an inappropriate behavior that has been going on for some time. *Warning your child keeps you from appearing arbitrary, but it is extremely important to follow through with consequences the very next time the behavior occurs. The goal is to get your child to stop with the warning.*

The way most parents get into trouble with warnings is that they give them again and again without following through with their threat. This teaches children things their parents don't intend—that they aren't "good for their word" and that ignoring is the way to respond to commands. Sometimes children don't listen well. You can tell them to stop over and over again, and redirect their attention, but they just keep at it; then something else needs to be done. Some experts will tell you never to give children warnings, just to put them in time-out immediately, but everyone knows it is easy to miss what someone has said, to not have it "register." I think if a behavior is more annoying than it is dangerous, and if the child can understand what you are saying, he can be given a warning. Tell him, "If you don't stop, you will go to time-out," or "If you do it again, I will take that away from you." However, to be fair about giving a warning, you must be very clear about what it is you want your child to stop doing and what will happen if he doesn't.

In order to truly be a warning, your statement must promise a consequence. "Stop running in the hall" is not a warning, it is a command. It doesn't tell what will happen if she doesn't stop. "If you don't stop, you will sit in time-out" is a warning. Once you have said what will happen if it continues, ignoring further misbehavior teaches your child that you don't mean what you say and that your warning is not to be taken seriously. In order to be effective, you *must* follow through with your consequences once you have drawn the line.

On the next page is a chart of when to use warnings. Notice that a warning should not be used when the child breaks a safety rule he knows and understands well. Running toward a busy street is a behavior that requires an immediate time-out. Likewise, you can't afford to give a warning to a child who is hurting another child. "Stop hitting her on the head or I will put you in time-out" is ridiculous because the other child will get hurt while you wait for yours to comply. In this situation, tell your child, "No, don't hit," and put him directly into time-out. In all situations not involving a safety rule, you can probably afford to give a warning. Tell your child, "If you don't stop (or 'If you do that again'), I will put you in time-out." Then do it the very next time you see the behavior.

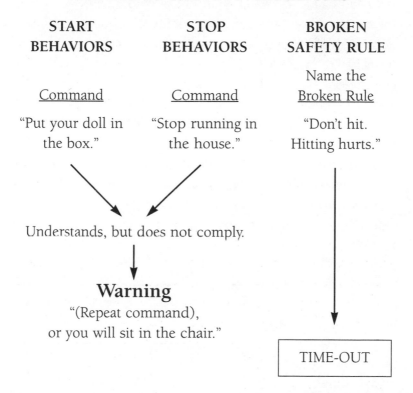

"WARNING OF TIME-OUT" PROCEDURES

START BEHAVIORS	STOP BEHAVIORS	BROKEN SAFETY RULE
		Name the
Command	Command	Broken Rule
"Put your doll in the box."	"Stop running in the house."	"Don't hit. Hitting hurts."

Understands, but does not comply.

Warning
"(Repeat command),
or you will sit in the chair."

TIME-OUT

A Crawler, of course, won't understand a warning. At this developmental level, simply say, "No, don't touch," in a firm but not loud tone of voice. If your child doesn't stop, repeat it again, but this time *get up*. Move him somewhere else or hand him a different object to play with. Eventually your Crawler will learn that your tone of voice is a warning in itself, and that you are going to move him if he doesn't stop, but he cannot be expected to understand this right away. Give him something appropriate to do so you can reinforce his behavior. This will help him learn to find the alternative activities himself.

There is one problem with warnings: It is difficult to know how long to wait for your child to comply before giving the consequence. For example, let's say you want your Talker to pick up some toys. You kneel next to her (so you know she hears you) and say, "Okay, it is time to put the truck away." She continues playing with the truck. How long to wait is a judgment call. Some parents choose to count out loud before acting on their threat. "If you don't pick up that truck by the count of five, you will sit in time-out. One . . . two . . . " This method can work, and may give your child more of a sense of control over when he chooses to act. However, giving a lengthy warning can teach your child that you will allow him just a little longer to comply, and your child may learn to require it every time.

	Walkers	Talkers and Threes
	Child eats appropriately.	
Create a Positive Environment	Parents comment about how nicely he is eating, and say things like, "Is that sandwich good?"	Parents give specific comments about how he is sitting or using utensils. They say things like, "You're eating a good supper tonight."

	Walkers	Talkers and Threes
Child waves sandwich in the air.		
Ignore Misbehavior	Parents keep talking to each other without acknowledging the behavior.	Parents keep talking to each other without acknowledging the behavior.
Child waves sandwich in the air more vigorously.		
Distract or Redirect	Parents comment on something having to do with the sandwich in his hand, like, "Do you have cheese in that sandwich?"	Parents comment on something to cause him to look at the sandwich in his hand, like, "Did I put ketchup on your sandwich?"
Child examines sandwich, then waves it around as if to throw it.		
Tell to Stop and Redirect	Parents tell him what *not* to do: "Don't throw," and what *to do:* "Put it on your plate and put some ketchup on it."	Parents tell him what *not* to do: "Don't throw," and what *to do:* "Cut it in squares and see how it looks."
Child postures as if to throw sandwich.		
Warn of Consequences	Parents tell what will happen if the behavior continues: "Don't throw or I'll take the sandwich."	Parents tell what will happen if the behavior continues: "If you throw that, you will sit in time-out."

Use Time-Out

Time-out means taking something positive away, including the attention of others, as a way of reducing a behavior. But time-out is not punishment; it does not include spankings or whippings. It isn't jail or solitary confinement, and it isn't meant to be a convenience for parents who want to get their kids out of their hair for a long period of time. Like the other steps on the Progressive Discipline continuum, time-out is a teaching tool. When parents use it correctly, they follow it with an opportunity for their child to behave well so they can reinforce the appropriate behavior. Another crucial part of using time-out in discipline is making sure its type and length fit a child's developmental level. When your child is young, taking away days of television, sending him to his room for an hour, or promising that he will not go to a friend's house the next week won't teach your child the right way to behave. When your child is young, time-out needs to last only long enough to give him the message that your attention (or his toy or some forbidden object) has been taken away for a while. The duration must be short enough that he can try again to behave appropriately before he forgets why he is in time-out. *The younger your child, the more immediate time-out and the opportunity to "do it right" must be.*

Let's start with Crawlers, since they begin to get into things as soon as they can move about in their environment. Imagine a Crawler who insists on pulling on her parents' curtains. Beside the fact that a parent might choose to move the curtains, this could be an opportunity to teach the Crawler to stop when told, "No," by moving her away from the curtains after it is said. Many people are surprised that removing a Crawler from the curtain is actually a form of time-out. You wouldn't give a warning to the Crawler because he wouldn't understand it, but you could tell him, "No," redirect him to an alternative object or activity, or move him to a different location if he doesn't take the suggestion. This is time-out from attention and the reinforcement of tugging on the curtain. He may not understand it as such, but it will have the eventual effect of teaching him to stop when he is told to do so. An older child can be returned to the vicinity of the curtains after a brief time-out and given a chance to behave appropriately. However, a Crawler will not remember the rule; he will need to be redirected again and again.

I once ate lunch with a Walker about eighteen months old who sat on a tall stool next to me. She crawled to her knees on her stool whenever the attention at the table was not focused on her, purposely threatening to stand up. Ignoring this behavior didn't work, since I was afraid she was going to fall, and redirecting her attention succeeded only temporarily. I decided to warn her that, if she continued to climb on her seat, I would put her on the floor. I knew there was nothing to do down there, and that she would not like the lack of attention or food. She sat up quickly, grinned at me the next time I looked her way, and climbed to her knees on the stool again! I immediately stood up, lifted her calmly from her stool, and placed her on the floor. The adults at the table continued their conversation, and she stood up within seconds to beg to come back up. I lifted her onto her stool and told her to sit in her seat, which she did compliantly the rest of the meal.

Many parents think that time-out must be done in a chair or down the hall in the child's room. Actually, *with young children, time-out must be so immediate that it is best done right in the room where the misbehavior occurred.* Young children's memories are very short. They will not sit in time-out and think about what they did wrong. The effectiveness of the technique is in the insult of being removed from something that was pleasurable. Its effect is most potent in the first few seconds after time-out begins. The younger the child, the shorter her attention span. Therefore, it is also important to end time-out quickly, before she finds something reinforcing with which to distract herself. The goal is to stop the misbehavior and encourage an appropriate behavior that can be reinforced. The purpose is to teach, not to punish.

You may have heard the rule that says not to leave a child in time-out longer than one minute for every year of his age. In general, that's a useful guideline, but it breaks down a little at the very youngest ages. A minute is too long to leave a Walker in time-out. You are likely to see additional misbehavior, and your child is likely to forget why he is there. You will have missed the teaching moment. Instead, put him in time-out just a few feet away, on the floor or on a chair or a couch nearby. Say, for example, "We don't hit." If he cries, ignore it. Don't worry if a Walker gets out of time-out. The main goal is to teach him not to do whatever you put him there for and give him a chance to behave appropriately. Moving him away from the setting is annoying to him. It will make your point. Don't frustrate yourself by making him sit in the chair and starting a whole new battle. Simply reinforce his appropriate behavior once he gets up.

For a Talker, the story gets a little more complicated. At this stage, you will want to teach him that restriction from his previous activity is the consequence of his behavior, and a ten-second sit a few feet away may not be enough. Use a chair or a couch that is a short distance from things that are reinforcing—people, television, or toys—and have him sit there a minute or two. Keep your comments beforehand simple and brief like, "We don't hit. Now sit here until I say you can get up," and avoid conversation, or even eye contact, while he is in time-out. A child this age may try to argue with you, blame someone else, or get in a discussion about what happened. He hit; you saw it; that's all you need to know. Save any discussion until later. If he gets out of his chair, put him back. However, soon after you put him there, find a reason to let him up. His attention span is still short; he isn't going to learn by sitting for a long time. Tell him he can get up *before* he crawls out of the chair. Make it look like *your* idea, that *you* were in control of the situation. If he gets up when you aren't looking, put him back. If he sits for a minute without trying to get up, say, "You can get up now, but remember, don't hit." If he is wailing, wait for him to take a deep breath and say, "Good, you stopped crying. You can get up now, but remember, don't hit."

This approach gives your child a chance to get back to square one with you and behave differently the next time around. Be sure to tell him a minute or two later—if he is behaving appropriately—that you like the way he is playing. If he repeats the behavior that got him into time-out, repeat the process. This can sometimes take an hour or more with a child who is really pushing the limits, but don't let him win. Remember the effect of occasional reinforcement. You started the process, finish it. Help him by giving alternative activities once he is out of time-out, but by all means, put him back in if he doesn't comply. *Young children are likely to forget why they are in time-out, or to find something else reinforcing to do while they are there. Your role is to put your child there at the right time, be in charge of when he gets out, and reward him afterward as soon as he engages in an appropriate behavior.*

For Threes, the story changes a little again. A Three is much better able to understand the rules and can be expected to stay in time-out until told to get up. Remember that you need to be in control of the situation. Tell him, "You didn't stop running, now you will sit in the chair. Stay here until I say you can get up." Then ignore him. Any attention you give him at this point will be reinforcing. Ignore all yelling, complaining, crying, threats of hating you or of throwing up, and simply let him sit there for a few minutes. If he gets up out of the chair, put him back, saying, "Stay in the chair. If you get up again, I will hold you in the chair." Then, if he gets up again, get down behind the chair where he won't be reinforced by looking at your face, cross his arms over his chest, and hold his hands, one in each of yours. In this position, he will not be able to get up or bite no matter how much he struggles. He may still call out obnoxious things, but he won't be able to leave the chair or to hurt you. A struggle in this position can go on for a long time, so get comfortable. Your immediate goal is now to teach him to stay in the chair so you can use it for any future time-out situations. As soon as you feel your child relax even slightly, tell him "Good, you stayed in the chair. You can get up now, but, remember, don't run." There isn't any sense in making him stay longer at this point. Time-out was the consequence for running. In his struggle to get out of the chair, he has long since forgotten his misbehavior. Let him up when he relaxes and repeat the teaching points: he sat still, he can get up, and you don't want him to run any more.

If you are just beginning to use time-out with your child and he is at least a Talker or a Three, role-play it a few times with him when he hasn't actually done anything wrong. In therapy, I do this with the parents and child together. I have the child bring a stuffed animal to the session and ask him, "Does your animal ever do anything you wish he wouldn't do?" Children almost always say yes; and they almost always name a behavior their parents are trying to get them to stop! If a child can't come up with a behavior to work on with his stuffed animal, I tell him I will help his animal not bite any more. This is a simple example a child can understand. To help familiarize him with the time-out process, I run through it using a warning (even though I tell the parents not to give a warning for biting because biting is hurtful to others).

I have the child make his stuffed animal bite my hand. "Ouch," I cry. "Don't bite me." (I skip the part about distracting the animal to get him to do something appropriate). Then the animal bites me again. "Ouch," I say. "Don't bite. If you bite me again, I will put you in the chair." The animal, of course, bites again, and I put it in the chair. "Now stay there until I say you can get out." I wait a minute, then let the animal up. "You can get up now," I say, "but remember, don't bite."

I run through this exercise again, showing the child what to do if his animal decides to yell things from the chair (we ignore it) or get up. If it gets up, we put it back, saying, "If you get up again, I will hold you in the chair." Then, when it gets up, I crouch behind the chair, cross its arms, and hold it in the chair. When it sits still for a brief moment, I tell it, "Good, you stayed in the chair. You can get up now, but remember, don't bite."

The child, of course, thinks this is very funny, but he gets to learn the routine without being in trouble, and he knows that his parents, who are sitting in the room, know it, too. You might run through this during a playtime with your child, just to give him a jump on the situation. It may save you some explaining—or having to demonstrate the procedure for the first time during an actual incident later.

On the next page is a chart of time-out procedures. Notice that there are three ways on the chart for a child to end up in time-out, and only two of them involve giving a warning. Safety violations should always result in immediate time-out to teach that the behavior was dangerous and not acceptable. The other two situations, one in which you want to get the child to

"TIME-OUT" PROCEDURES

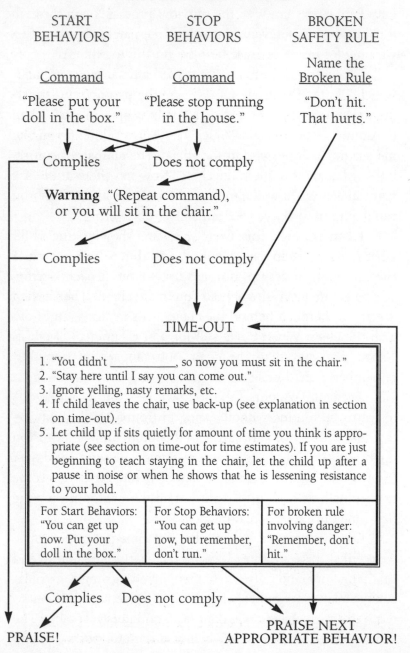

START
BEHAVIORS

STOP
BEHAVIORS

BROKEN
SAFETY RULE

Command

"Please put your
doll in the box."

Command

"Please stop running
in the house."

Name the
Broken Rule

"Don't hit.
That hurts."

Complies   Does not comply

Warning "(Repeat command),
or you will sit in the chair."

Complies   Does not comply

TIME-OUT

1. "You didn't _____, so now you must sit in the chair."
2. "Stay here until I say you can come out."
3. Ignore yelling, nasty remarks, etc.
4. If child leaves the chair, use back-up (see explanation in section on time-out).
5. Let child up if sits quietly for amount of time you think is appropriate (see section on time-out for time estimates). If you are just beginning to teach staying in the chair, let the child up after a pause in noise or when he shows that he is lessening resistance to your hold.

For Start Behaviors:	For Stop Behaviors:	For broken rule
"You can get up now. Put your doll in the box."	"You can get up now, but remember, don't run."	involving danger: "Remember, don't hit."

Complies   Does not comply

PRAISE!

PRAISE NEXT
APPROPRIATE BEHAVIOR!

start doing something and one in which you want to get him to *stop* doing something annoying, are situations in which you can give a warning. But remember that *a warning must only be given once.* Don't say, "If I catch you running in the hall three more times, you are going to sit in time-out!" Your child must understand that when you give a warning, you will follow through with time-out the very next time you see the behavior occur.

Time-out is most effective at getting a child to *stop* doing something he isn't supposed to be doing. It also works in situations where you are trying to get your child to *start* doing something he refuses to do. However, because you are likely to be in a hurry when you want your child to do something like putting on her coat or picking up her toys, this might not be the best situation in which to use time-out for the first time. If you can afford to wait for her to tantrum or return her to time-out several times, go ahead and use it, then request the behavior again as soon as he is allowed to get up. However, if you think your child may put up a struggle, use time-out first for behaviors you want to stop and get her used to the routine, then extend it to situations in which you want her to begin doing something.

Time-out should:

- ◆ be immediate (for dangerous behavior) OR
- ◆ follow a warning (immediately after the next violation of the rule)
- ◆ be brief
- ◆ be matter of fact, firm
- ◆ not involve discussion on the way there, or responding while there
- ◆ be followed by a reminder of the behavior that put him there
- ◆ be followed by praise for the next "good" behavior

	Walkers	*Talkers and Threes*
	Child eats appropriately.	
Create a Positive Environment	Parents comment about how nicely he is eating, and say things like, "Is that sandwich good?"	Parents give specific comments about how he is sitting or using utensils. They say things like, "You're eating a good supper tonight."
	Child waves sandwich in the air.	
Ignore Misbehavior	Parents keep talking to each other without acknowledging the behavior.	Parents keep talking to each other without acknowledging the behavior.
	Child waves sandwich in the air more vigorously.	
Distract or Redirect	Parents comment on something having to do with the sandwich in his hand, like, "Do you have cheese in that sandwich?"	Parents comment on something to cause him to look at the sandwich in his hand, like, "Did I put ketchup on your sandwich?"
	Child examines sandwich, then waves it around as if to throw it.	
Tell to Stop and Redirect	Parents tell him what *not* to do: "Don't throw," and what *to* do: "Put it on your plate and put some ketchup on it."	Parents tell him what *not* to do: "Don't throw," and what *to* do: "Cut it in squares and see how it looks."

	Walkers	Talkers and Threes
	Child postures as if to throw sandwich.	
Warn of Consequence	Parents tell what will happen if the behavior continues: "Don't throw or I'll take the sandwich."	Parents tell what will happen if the behavior continues: "If you throw that, you will sit in time-out."
	Child throws the sandwich.	
Time-out for Misbehavior	Parents repeat the rule: "I said 'don't throw.'" They remove the sandwich for 15 seconds, then return it saying: "Here's your sandwich. Now remember, don't throw." Parents give a distracting task and reward the next appropriate behavior.	Parents repeat the rule: "I said, 'don't throw.' Now sit here until I say you can get up." Parents put the child in time-out for 30 seconds, then return him to the table, repeating the rule: "Now don't throw your food." They give a distracting task and reward the next appropriate behavior.

Natural Opportunities to Teach

THERE ARE MANY OPPORTUNITIES to use what you have learned about reinforcement and progressive discipline. Since these are teaching tools, they can also be used for situations that don't involve misbehavior, for 1) guiding learning, 2) minimizing power struggles, 3) making smooth transitions from one activity to another, and 4) teaching your child to wait.

Guide Learning

Since you are now comfortable with positive reinforcement, you will be using it to reinforce appropriate behaviors whenever your child does them, but taking this principle one step further, you can also use it to increase behaviors your child doesn't necessarily do *on purpose*. Young children can sometimes learn behaviors by literally being "taken through the motions." This is not surprising since you can see this happen with older children and even adults. A Little League player understands how to swing a bat more effectively when he is physically guided through a few strokes and can feel what it is like to hit the ball. A gymnast first learns a back handspring using a belt around his waist that is connected by ropes to two spotters. When he "gets the feel of it," he knows what he will be trying to do it without the belt. If a young child is developmentally ready to learn a new skill, you can help him in a similar way: Show him how to put blocks into a cup by placing his hand around the block and loosening his grasp on the block when it is over the cup. This is the same principle you are using when you hold your child in his chair until he relaxes during time-out, then praise him for staying there. You are guiding his learning by showing him the behavior you want him to exhibit.

Guided learning can also apply when you are trying to get your child to start a behavior like picking up her toys. If she hesitates or doesn't understand, you can guide her learning by taking her through the motions rather than expecting her to start doing it on her own. First, in order for her to learn to do this herself, she must know what you want her to do. "Pick up your room" may not have meaning to her. "Pick up this truck" does. Second, be sure the task you are requesting is within her capabilities. Don't expect her to clean her room on her own. No Talker or Three is going to stick with a task more than a few minutes, even with direction. Finally, direct each step. Tell her, "Put the truck in the basket." When she complies, praise her, and move on to the next toy until you have done this for several toys. Then consider the job done.

If you tell your Three to put her truck in the box and she says "No," or walks away, you are going to want to insure that she complies. You could simply threaten, "If you don't pick up your toy, you will sit in the chair." That may succeed in getting compliance, especially if you keep the time-out short and repeat the command when she gets up, but if you are in a hurry, you may not have time to put your child back in time-out several times to get her to comply. If she isn't familiar with time-out, she could get distracted by the whole process rather than learn from your discipline. Instead, simply tell her, "if you don't pick it up, I will *help* you do it."

"Help" in this case does not mean doing it *all* for her, it means taking her little arm through the motion (without hurting her) so you can praise her behavior—even though she didn't mean to do it! Reach her hand down, grasp the truck, and drop it into the box. Act as though she did it on purpose. Take your hand away and say, "Good, you put the truck in the box. Now put the doll in the box." Do this same routine for several toys, and your child will probably put one in the box herself. After two or three toys, thank her for her help, and dismiss her. You were going to have to pick up the toys anyway. Let her leave believing that she helped. Remember that your goal is to teach. Because she now knows what you mean and that you mean business, she will be more likely to comply in the future.

Give Some Control

Power struggles are about—that's right—power. Children do not like to feel that they are out of control of a situation any more than parents do. All of us like to feel that we can affect the things that happen to us, positive or negative. As soon as children are old enough to realize that there are options, they like to choose what to eat, what to play with, and where to go in the house. This does not mean any choice should be allowed; a child should not choose *whether* to go to bed or *whether* to go with the family in the car—they still need boundaries and rules. One way to lower the number of struggles you have over your requests is to offer your child two options that still accomplish your goal but help him to feel he has had a choice. He could, for example, choose whether to take his stuffed animal or his doll to bed; or whether to dress in the green or blue slacks before leaving in the car.

Make Smooth Transitions

Giving choices to a child can be very helpful in getting him to move from one setting to another. These transitions can be difficult when your child is engrossed in his play and does not feel he has finished his activity in one setting before it is time to go to the next one. If a child's work is not complete and stopping is not his idea, he may have difficulty thinking about anything else at that particular time. I watched a woman stand in a doorway with her child's coat, yelling at him to hurry up. Her child ignored her until she yanked him up by one arm. Instead of having this altercation, this mother could have gotten down at her child's level, shown interest in what he was doing, and introduced the fact that they were going to go do something else. "I think I'll get some orange juice," or, "I'll bet Grandma is sitting at her window wondering when we are going to get there" are effective ways to get a child to think leaving is a good idea (in fact, even *his* idea) without creating a fuss. The goal is to help your child shift his attention from one activity to the next. This is a learned skill and your efforts working with your child now will help him to do this more easily as he grows older. Transitions are discussed more in the section on "Getting Ready to Go Somewhere" (page 181).

Teach How to Wait

Because saying "No" to a child's requests is usually easier than complying, many parents say "No" quickly whenever their child asks for things. Sometimes they do it when they might have said "Yes" if they had thought about it for a moment, and by the time they decide they were too harsh and change their mind, they have a screaming child on their hands. Instead of teaching that Dad or Mom can be reasonable and change their decisions once in a while, this tells a child that crying is the way to get what he or she wants.

There are several other reasons to say "Yes" to your child's requests if you can, before he or she begins to tantrum. First, requests generally are simple ones, like "Pick me up" or "Play with me." These can be satisfied with just a brief interaction, which helps build a positive environment. Second, saying "Yes" can give you an opportunity to introduce a delay in responding to requests. In essence, you can use it to teach your child to wait. When my children were very young, I responded positively to their requests whenever I could. This pleased them and of course was easier than listening to them whine when I said "No;" there certainly were enough of those times as well. With time, I imposed a contingency on the behaviors they requested. For example, I would answer, "Can I have a cookie" with a response that involved a very brief delay: "Yes, *wait* while I get it out of the cupboard." Using judgment about how long my child had learned to wait patiently, I would take twenty or thirty seconds to get it out of the cupboard and make sure she wasn't fussing when I gave it to her. As my children got older, I was able to lengthen the delay in my response by answering questions like, "Can I have a glass of milk" with, "Yes, I'll get it as soon as I finish setting the table." At bedtime they learned to wait for their request for a story to be read by my saying, "Yes. You wait in your bed while I put these clothes away." When I was interrupted while talking to others, I would say, "I'll listen to you as soon as I finish talking."

In each of these situations, my children learned to wait longer and longer periods of time to get what they requested. This varied with their developmental stage, of course. You will have to be the judge of how long your child can wait. If she has never waited patiently for fifteen seconds, don't make her wait five minutes. Her ability to wait must be built up gradually. If you can set it up so that she succeeds in waiting quietly for a brief period of time the desired object or activity will reinforce her *waiting* rather than her *whining*. Below are some guidelines for how long a child can typically wait and examples of types of requests that can be used as teaching opportunities.

TEACHING TO WAIT				
Stage	Type of request	Suggested type of response	How long your child can wait	How to know when you have succeeded
Baby or Crawler	Usually communicated by unintentional behavior.	Interact with your child while you figure out his need.	Does not wait.	Fussing ceases.
Walker	"More milk?"	"Yes. You wait while I get it from the fridge."	10 seconds.	Waits happily with anticipation.
Talker	"Can I have more milk?"	"Yes. You wait while I cut your meat. You eat a few bites while I get the milk from the fridge."	1–2 minutes.	Complies with your request.
Three	"Will you read me this book?"	"Yes. You wait while I put these groceries away, then I will read."	3–5 minutes.	Waits patiently.

If your child is having a difficult time waiting for you to provide whatever he has requested, you might want to include a distraction activity. "I'll read your book as soon as I put these groceries away" may be easier for him to tolerate if you suggest, "Here, put these cans on the shelf," or "You look at the pictures while I put these groceries away." This can be particularly useful with Walkers and Talkers. The important thing is that you are slowly teaching him that he doesn't have to have his needs met immediately. He can occupy himself briefly as long as you follow through with your promise.

It isn't possible to say "Yes" to every request; doing this would not teach your child the realities of the world. There will be plenty of times when you have to refuse a request for a cookie before dinner or a request to play outside. Save "No" for those times, and really mean it. Do your very best not to change your mind later, because you may reinforce whining or crying and definitely not earn trust points. Remember that intermittently reinforced behaviors can be very, very difficult to get rid of. "No" should mean "No." Make sure you mean it when you say it.

Make It Fun

No one would want to work or live in an environment where things were serious all the time; your child shouldn't have to, either. At the risk of sounding like Mary Poppins, it really is true that things go better, faster, and more pleasantly if you sometimes make them into a game. Be playful. Watch the tone of your voice. Sounding tired, irritated, or angry can teach a child that you are not someone who is pleasant to be with, and, worse yet, teach her to behave the same way. Playing with a child doesn't take a lot of effort: Just sit with her and comment on what *she* is doing if you don't have energy to be active yourself. Be the road for her toy car, her partner at a tea party. Practice *following* your child's actions and commenting on them. She will be delighted at the attention, and you will build a very important relationship. When you are tired, suggest that she teach her stuffed animal some of the things she just learned or that she park her car in the "garage" under the couch.

Often, children respond to a request that includes an impish comment like, "Bet I'll get my coat on first" faster than they will to a serious command like, "Get your coat on, now." Being playful with your child is part of creating a positive environment, and it makes your attention even more important to him. This is a key factor in using any of the discipline techniques further down the progressive continuum. Playing with your child can keep you from taking things (or yourself) too seriously and can break the tension in a busy day. Having fun is part of showing your child respect: Seeing you smile and laugh tells him that you value your time together.

Tokens as Teaching Tools

WHILE THEY ARE LEARNING how to behave, children often do things that don't help them get along well in the world. Some behaviors are harmful, like hurting other children, and others are simply annoying. Most misbehavior can be handled using Progressive Discipline techniques, but sometimes misbehaviors happen so frequently that things seem totally out of control. When misbehaviors are really entrenched, it can take a long time before your child figures out there is a payoff for behaving the right way. If he is a Talker or a Three, a token reward system may help you both focus on the positive behaviors you want to increase. This process involves giving tokens (stars, check marks, stickers, etc.) for behaviors that don't happen as frequently as you would like—anything from doing chores to saying please and thank you. When done appropriately, giving tokens each time the desired behavior happens increases the behavior.

Many people who try a token reward system see little or no improvement in their child's behavior, or the change is only temporary, and sometimes this happens because of errors in technique: The token system wasn't used properly. However, this also can happen when tokens are used without understanding Progressive Discipline or the key ingredients of effective parenting. When a token reward system is used correctly—with commitment, respect, trustworthiness, and the right technique—it can shorten the time a behavior takes to improve and promote a permanent change.

Before you decide to start giving tokens for every good behavior, here are several words of caution: First, you can't address every behavior your child does with a token reward system. Having more than one going on at the same time will water down your effectiveness, and keeping track of all the behaviors you are giving tokens for will confuse and frustrate you. A token system must be applied with care and forethought. Keep *recognizing and praising* the other good behaviors your child does. Save the token system for a specific behavior on which you want to focus.

The second caution about any token system is that it must be carried out consistently. Starting to give tokens for certain behaviors and then missing opportunities or simply forgetting about it is like breaking a promise to your child. You will not earn trust points, and your child's behaviors may worsen. The token system will fail.

Other mistakes are easy to make with token systems, too. One parent told me her child's day-care teacher complained every day that three-and-one-half-year-old Ryan was naughty at the center. His mother wasn't sure exactly what he was doing wrong, but the teacher seemed to expect her to do something about it. She told Ryan that she would give him a star every day when she picked him up if he "had a good day." The teacher reported back to her each afternoon, and, for a day or two, things got a lot better (although Ryan's mother wasn't sure why). By the end of the week, though, Ryan's teacher was complaining again, and Ryan no longer seemed to care about the stars.

This system failed for several reasons. First, Ryan's teacher wasn't clear with Mrs. Jones (and perhaps herself) about what Ryan needed to do differently. If the adults couldn't identify it, Ryan wasn't likely to know, either. Second, even if Ryan sometimes did improve his behavior, he wasn't being rewarded soon enough to know he had done the right thing. Being rewarded at the end of the day was too long to wait for Ryan to connect it with what he had done during the day. The other reason this system failed was that Ryan liked stars, but not that much. After a day or two, he got bored. They were just sticky pieces of paper, and they didn't interest him any more than play money would interest an adult. Like the coins in your pocket, tokens should be symbols that mean something else can be purchased with them. To be effective, tokens must be exchangeable for other things that can't be given right away but are truly reinforcing.

Another mother, Ms. Smith, did things differently with her reward system. She wanted her daughter, Bailey, to get used to sitting on the potty so she could move ahead with toilet training. Bailey loved marshmallows and would sit on the potty for a few moments if one were offered as a reward, but Ms. Jones didn't want to give her too many, and marshmallows weren't practical to carry around. To solve this problem, she decided to use stickers as token rewards for sitting on the potty. She promised Bailey a marshmallow whenever she got ten stickers, but her system didn't work. Bailey was only sixteen months old—too young to be doing potty training or using a token system. She didn't care about the stickers or understand the chart, and she cried for marshmallows every time she sat on the potty.

As with any discipline technique, your child's developmental level will determine whether a token system is appropriate. Token systems use symbols (tokens) to signal that a reinforcer will be available later. In order to understand how tokens work, a child must have basic symbolic reasoning ability, which usually develops late in the Talker stage (ages twenty-four to thirty-six months). At this age, children are able to put words together and count a few objects. Both skills show that they are using symbols—words—for the objects they represent. Your child will not understand a token reward system until he or she reaches this point.

> Before beginning a token reward system, ask yourself the following questions and be sure to share your answers to the questions with any other individuals who will be caring for or rewarding your child:
>
> 1. What specific behavior do you want to change?
> 2. Is it reasonable to expect your child to do it?
> 3. What type of token is best for your child?
> 4. How should your child earn tokens?
> 5. What will your child be saving the tokens for?
> 6. Will you be rewarding the presence or absence of a behavior?
> 7. Can you do this system effectively?
> 8. When will you discontinue the system?

What Behavior Do You Want to Change?

An effective token reward system requires that you decide ahead of time what behavior you want to change. Can you describe the behavior? Can you count the times it happens? If you told someone else to reward it also, would he or she know when it occurred and reward it exactly the same as you would? Behaviors like "being good" are not specific enough. If you had a new job and were told that your job was to "be good," you wouldn't know exactly what that meant. It could mean standing on your head or running around the room! Even if you knew *generally* what it meant—like talking to customers on the phone—you wouldn't know how good was good enough. You wouldn't know how many calls you were supposed to make, how often, or how long you should talk. Would it be "good" if you stayed on the phone all day? Would it be "not good" if you got off the phone to use the restroom? Your child can't know what "good" means, either, unless you tell him. If it means hanging up his coat, standing quietly in line, or brushing his teeth, say so. Then focus on just one of these behaviors first.

Even if you know what you want your child to do, a behavior can be difficult to describe, and your child may not be able to tell when he is doing it right. Whining is a good example. Is asking three times for something whining? Is raising the pitch of his voice? What about crying? Since you will want to reward your child when he is not whining, you must know when the behavior occurs and when it doesn't. If he only whines when you are fixing dinner, giving tokens when he is playing in his room that afternoon (but not whining) probably won't teach him about not whining when it is likely to occur. This is not the situation in which he typically whines. Giving him tokens while he is playing in his room may increase his play behaviors, but it won't reduce whining when he wants a cookie from the cupboard.

In this situation, you may want to specifically reward your child for *asking for things without whining.* If this happens so rarely that you can't find an instance when he doesn't whine to reward him for, you may need to prompt or model the behavior you want. When he whines to get something, say, "Don't whine," then demonstrate the way you want him to ask for things. Tell him in a calm, conversational tone, "May I have a cookie, please?" Then reward him with a token when he says it like you did.

Is It Reasonable to Expect Your Child to Do It?

If your child is a Talker or a Three and seems to understand the concept of earning tokens for something he wants to have later, he probably can handle a token reward system, but you must be sure he can actually do the expected behavior. If he *never* does it, you won't be able to reward him for it, and the system will fail. If he is very young, for example, he may not be able to do all the steps necessary to get a reward for something like brushing his teeth or cleaning his room. He may be too easily distracted or not able to think of it on his own. Set the situation up for your child to succeed, reward him for simpler steps that lead up to the final behavior. Prompt the next step as he finishes a step: "Good, you have your toothbrush. Now put the toothpaste on it." If these behaviors are too difficult, put the toothpaste on his toothbrush, hand it to him, and let him brush. *Then* reward him for "brushing his teeth."

Likewise, don't expect your child to clean his room to your usual standards on his own. He will need help knowing what you want and staying on task, and he will need to experience success. Try cleaning his room ahead of time (you'd have to anyway), leaving just a few articles of clothing on the floor. Tell him to put them down the clothes chute or in his drawer, and when he does, reward him for "cleaning his room." With time, he will be able to do more steps on his own, but during these early years, you must shape his behavior. Give him something he can actually accomplish and reward it heartily.

What Type of Token Is Best?

Most tokens lose their appeal after just a few days; then children will work for them only because they are exchangeable for other things. However, using a token your child likes in the first place can help get the system off the ground and keep his interest longer. Stickers that are colorful or shiny work well. Along with their visual appeal, they can offer your child a sense of control as he sticks them onto a chart to mark his progress toward his goal, or he can simply make check marks with colored pens or markers.

Some children like more concrete tokens than stars or check marks. They like having something they can hold in their hands and feel, look at, or play with. Your child may prefer to earn large washers or bolts (large ones that he can't choke on) or even poker chips. Any of these three-dimensional tokens is better than money itself, since young children can't add high enough to get to any real buying power. Have the reward, if it is one you must purchase, available in the closet for him to "buy" with however many tokens you have decided it will take. Pick tokens you can carry around in your pocket so you can give them quickly when they are earned. Finally, make sure your child likes whatever tokens you choose; otherwise, he may not work for them long enough to learn that you will actually follow through with the bigger reward.

How Should Tokens Be Earned?

At some point, your child will be able to count her tokens the way an adult counts money, but at two or three years of age, she won't be able to count very high. Don't make the number of tokens required so high that she struggles to count them accurately or can't earn enough to "buy a reward" fairly quickly. She will lose interest if she must wait more than a day to trade them in for a reward. For Talkers, the easiest type of chart is one with only a small number of boxes in it, usually ten or twelve at the most. Fill one box with a star or check mark each time the desired behavior occurs, and when all boxes are filled, allow your child to trade the tokens for her reward. Tokens like poker chips can be collected in a jar or a bag, or laid out on a chart on her dresser. If your child needs help counting, try using an egg carton (or half of one) into which she can place her tokens as she collects them. When all six or twelve compartments are filled, give the reward. *Give her a token every time she does the desired behavior and give her the bigger reward as soon as she earns the required number of tokens.*

Giving a reward as soon as it's earned allows for the possibility that your child will not do what she is supposed to all the time, whatever the reason. She won't sit on the potty every time you ask, and she will forget to brush her teeth once in a while. The purpose of the token system is to increase her compliance by rewarding her for doing the right things, not to punish her for making a mistake. *Don't take tokens away for not doing the desired behavior;* simply remind her that she missed the chance for a token and you hope she will do it the next time. Don't require her to earn ten tokens by a deadline, either, and then take them away if she doesn't make it. If she realizes that making a mistake early in the day makes her goal impossible to achieve, she will have no incentive to work for tokens the rest of the day. If you set the system up for her to fill an egg crate with washers in order to get a reward, she may be upset when she has to turn them in for the reward. Try letting her keep the ones she has "spent" for the reward in a jar. She will enjoy watching the jar fill up, and you can offer a bigger reward when it does.

Token systems must be simple. Choose one or two behaviors you want to influence and give tokens only for those behaviors. Once you have begun, don't offer extra ways to earn points, require more tokens than originally stated, or offer extra tokens to encourage behaviors. Changes like these confuse parents as well as children. Use token systems as a means to an end, a way to change a specific behavior; don't make the technique more important than the outcome.

Since you are not going to be giving tokens forever, be sure to include attention and praise as well. Statements that encourage your child to feel good about the behaviors themselves can help your child learn to reward himself for similar behaviors in the future. Say, for example: "Don't you feel good that you brushed your teeth on your own?" or "You must be pretty proud of yourself for going in the potty."

What Should Tokens Be Exchanged For?

A token reward system that offers immediate reinforcement should keep your child motivated to earn more, at least for a while, but tokens lose their appeal quickly unless they can be traded for other things that have more lasting value. Talkers may need to be able to trade tokens in several times a day, by getting a small treat or prize each time ten tokens are earned. An older child can wait longer to receive a reward but should be able to earn something by the end of one day. This means you must make an educated guess about how often your child is likely to do the behavior so you know how many tokens to require for him to earn a reward.

In general, rewards should be extra treats or privileges your child doesn't typically get. If he is working to have a friend over, and friends come over anyway, your reward will lose its power. If you offer to take him to a particular movie if he earns a certain number of tokens, and he sees the movie at a birthday party, he won't work for that reward. There are many rewards you can offer in exchange for tokens. A child who is old enough to express an opinion may want to take part in deciding what to work for. Offer a variety of rewards that are worth different numbers of tokens or offer a new one the next time around, once a reward is earned, but never change the reward your child thinks he has earned, and definitely don't forget to give it to him.

Here are some rewards that have worked well in exchange for tokens:

- *Grab bags*—Try individually wrapping small prizes or trinkets that can be put together in a grab bag. When your child earns the required number of tokens, allow him to reach into the bag and choose a prize. If he claims not to like the prize he has drawn, offer to play with it with him, and tell him he will pull out something different the next time around. The element of surprise will keep him working for the other prizes, unless none of them are things that would interest him.

- *Outings*—Most children who use tokens will work for a chance to go to a movie, skating, or out to eat. But you don't need to choose something expensive to do; he won't know the difference between a walk to the park and going out to dinner as far as cost is concerned.

- *Friends*—By the time your child is a Three, he will enjoy the company of others. These social experiences are important to your child's development, and you will not want to require that he earn every contact with his friends. However, he may work very hard for tokens he can trade for an extra visit or outing with a friend.

(continued)

◆ *Treats*—Children love treats and often will work for a piece of gum or candy, or even cheese or cereal in exchange for a few tokens, but you will not want to give these things too often or use the token system too long. As always, be cautious of the danger of choking on these items.

◆ *Time with you*—To most children, this is the most reinforcing of all possible rewards, and it doesn't cost a thing. Remember that misbehaviors are often the result of insufficient positive attention. Tell your child he will earn "special time" with you after a certain number of tokens, and make it possible for him to earn enough tokens to do this at least once per day. Tell him that special time means you will do absolutely anything he wants you to do (within reason) during that time, that he will have your undivided attention while you play with his toys or watch him do somersaults. Even though you give him attention at other times, special time will seem truly important and unique if you set a timer for 15 minutes, get someone to watch your other children, ignore the phone, and put your child in charge during that time. Take it one step further with an older child and tell him he has earned this special time because his behavior has made it possible. Say, "When I don't have to use my time correcting your behavior, I have more time to spend with you."

What Should You Reward?

REWARDING THE PRESENCE OF A BEHAVIOR

When you are trying to increase the frequency of a behavior, whether it is getting dressed, brushing teeth, saying please, or telling the truth, it is important to reward it each time it occurs. The beauty of a token system is that you can mark your child's progress by giving a token when it isn't practical to give something the child wants right then. Of course, tokens should not take the place of compliments and praise. They work best if given together.

Below is an example of a chart for a Talker who is sometimes able to count to ten. She doesn't actually need to be able to count that high; the chart itself shows her how many more tokens she must earn to get the reward.

Sarah's Reward Chart for Sitting on the Potty

★	★			

Gets a star each time she sits for 5 seconds.
Gets a reward when the chart is full.

The chart on the next page helped three-year-old David remember to say "Please." He did it occasionally to begin with, but began to say it frequently after the token program started. His mother gave him a sticker each time he said it along with a request and required that he earn quite a few stickers before she gave the reward, fifteen minutes of "control time" with her. He worked hard for this privilege and earned it at least once per day.

David's Reward Chart for Saying "Please"

★	★	★	★	★
★				

Earns a sticker each time he says "please."
Gets a reward when the chart is full.

When Jason went to the dentist at three and a half, he was told he needed to brush his teeth. His parents set up a chart that gave him two chances per day to earn a token. Each time he brushed his teeth, he got a check mark on the chart. When he brushed his teeth both times in one day, he got a piggyback ride to bed. Each time he earned six tokens, he got a treat from a grab bag.

Jason's Reward Chart for Brushing His Teeth

	Mon.	Tues.	Wed.	Thurs.	Fri.	Sat.	Sun.
☀	✓	✓	✓	✓	Sixth check mark earns treat		
🌙		✓	✓				

Jason gets a check each time he brushes
his teeth and a treat after every 6th time.

REWARDING THE ABSENCE OF A BEHAVIOR

Although you may be tempted to tell your child what *not* to do a lot of the time, remember that most behaviors can be stated positively, so that your child is working *to* behave a certain way rather than *to not* behave a certain way. For example, "not getting out of bed" can be rephrased as "staying in bed." "Don't push while you are in line" can be phrased as "wait your turn." These particular misbehaviors have an opposite behavior that can be stated positively and easily rewarded. However, some behaviors, like "not hitting," don't have a single opposing behavior. You would have to reward *everything else* in order to decrease the misbehavior. As always, your child's many appropriate behaviors should be noticed and praised. However, the frequency of a specific misbehavior can sometimes be decreased by being offered a token for it not occurring during a specified period of time. In other words, a parent can reinforce the *absence* of the behavior. *A good way to reward your child for not doing a specific behavior is to break the day into parts and give a token if the behavior does not happen during that period of time.* This type of token system requires that your child understand the concept of being rewarded for *not* doing something and is best not used before your child is at least three years of age.

Rewarding the absence of a behavior such as hitting, for example, does not necessarily mean you should *ignore* your child when she does the behavior. At that point, you will probably need to put her in time-out or deliver whatever other contingency you have decided on. However, by offering tokens and praise following periods of time when she hasn't hit, you can call her attention to the fact that she hasn't done it for a while and reinforce her for not doing it. Break the day into several distinct parts, such as from when she gets up until breakfast, breakfast until lunch, lunch until dinner, and dinner until bedtime. At the end of a given time period, say, for example, "Let's see. It's lunchtime, time to think about whether you hit at all since breakfast. Nope. You did a great job! You *told* me you wanted to hit Sam for taking your truck but you didn't do it. You get a star! Keep up the good work."

If your child does hit, identify it when it occurs and send her to time-out. Say, "Kate, that is hitting. You must sit in time-out. Now you won't get your token at lunchtime." Then later, at lunch, say, "It's lunchtime, time to think about whether you hit at all since breakfast. Oh yes, you did hit Sam when he took your truck. No star this time. But we are starting a new time period from now until dinner. You'll get a star at dinner if you don't hit between now and then. I know you can do it." This process tells her how she is doing and what she needs to do differently, and puts her back at square one with you. Approaching her hitting this way fits with your parenting principles.

Some children seem to get into trouble for a multitude of rule infractions. When you are trying to reduce several misbehaviors by challenging your child not to do them, consider bolstering your use of time-out by rewarding your child for not having to be sent there during different periods of the day. When he misbehaves, remind him with each warning that if he is sent to time-out, he will also lose his token during that period of the day. The success of this system requires that you and your child know exactly what behaviors will land him in time-out and that you follow through with your discipline in a very consistent manner. At the beginning of each time period, be as specific as possible about the two or three behaviors you don't want to see: "If you hit, scratch, or bite anyone, you will go to time-out. If you don't do any of those things between now and lunch, you will get a star on this chart. As soon as you have six stars, you can reach into the grab bag and pull out a prize. I hope you can stay out of time-out by not hitting, scratching, or biting." Be sure to review his behavior at the end of every time period, and present the next time period as a chance to do as well or better. A "dry run" may help your child know exactly what will happen if he does the behaviors that you are targeting, and what you will do if he doesn't do them.

Can You Use Tokens Effectively?

I have already said that using a token reward system effectively requires good technique and that good technique

Robert's Chart for Not Needing Time-out

	Morning till Breakfast ☺	Breakfast till Lunch	Lunch till Dinner	Dinner till Bedtime
Monday	★	★		★
Tuesday				

Three out of four stars per day earns "Control Time."
When 10 stars are earned, Robert goes to a movie.

must be applied with commitment, respect, and trustworthiness. Promising a reward and then forgetting to give it is a sure way to make the system fail. Making an honest deal with your child that you will reward certain behaviors with tokens (and tokens with other prizes) is a great chance to show your child that your word is good. You will especially earn trust points for remembering to give the tokens if you think of them before your child has to ask for them. If a token reward system will be too difficult to use because it doesn't fit into your schedule right now, don't start it; wait until you have more time and energy to devote to it.

A token reward system is a matter of convenience. You can't carry a toy truck she has been wanting to the grocery store or soccer game, and you can't give her a new doll each time she brushes her teeth. Because they are "earned" like money and used to purchase things of greater value (including your time and attention), tokens can be both reinforcing and convenient. Pick a token that is safe, and, if you have other children, choose something they won't play with or spoil. If possible, tell your childcare worker and relatives about the system; if they have the same commitment, respect, trust-worthiness, and understanding of the technique, you may want them to give tokens to your child as well. When the people involved in your child's care are looking for and rewarding the same behaviors, your system will have greater success.

How Will You Stop Using the Tokens?

A token reward system is a handy way to quickly increase the frequency of certain desired behaviors. Because token systems tend to clearly define desired behaviors and motivate children to do them, they often accomplish what could take weeks or months to achieve simply through praise and attention. However, token systems are not intended to be a permanent part of your child's life. You will want to use them only when behaviors need an added boost and discontinue them soon after your child's behavior reaches the desired level.

Many parents are tempted to throw away the chart as soon as their child's behavior improves and to simply forget about it. Children are upset by this act and remember the disappointment the next time their parents want to set up a token system. They learn not to trust that their parents will follow through with any "deal" they offer. Unless your child *suggests* that you stop the system *because he thinks he doesn't need it anymore,* be cautious about ending it too abruptly.

If your child's behavior improves, and she seems to lose interest in the token system, tell her you are proud of her behavior, that you don't think she needs to use a chart anymore, and that you would be glad to stop after she finishes the current chart. If she has been earning time with you, be sure to tell her that you will continue to spend time with her frequently—and then do it. No matter how you stop the token system, it is important to talk to your child about it ahead of time. Say something like, "You are doing so well, let's just have our outings without using a chart." Or, "I've been keeping all the poker chips you bought your rewards with. If you do well this week, you can have them all to keep, and we'll stop."

Some parents prefer to fade out their token system instead of ending it all at once. This can give children continued attention for practicing their new behaviors before being expected to do them independently. If your child is doing well, wait until she earns a reward and you have paid it out, then negotiate a new reward that requires a few more tokens to be earned. Extend the required number of tokens she needs to earn her rewards, and/or have her work for different rewards that take a little longer. In either case, be sure to tell her what you will be doing: She will not appreciate thinking she has earned a reward only to find that she needs more tokens than she thought.

At the very end, be proud *with* your child that she doesn't need a token reward system anymore. Tell her how well she has done and why it has been a big help to you. As a final indication that you believe she can do this on her own, give her a few leftover charts to use while playing with her stuffed bear now that *she* doesn't need them anymore.

PART IV

Using What You Know

Different situations call for different approaches: You can't cross a river in a car or a desert in a canoe. It helps to know before you start out on your journey what kind of terrain you are likely to face and to be ready with the right tools. The same is true in parenting. You are most likely to choose the best techniques for your child's behaviors if you think ahead to the situations you will probably face. This chapter discusses the common problem situations you may encounter and the techniques that are most effective to use in them. Some situations will not come up until your child reaches the age of two or three years, if at all. Others are common to children of all ages. When it is important to approach a situation according to your child's stage of development, the techniques are presented according to the age at which they are most effective. When behaviors should not be considered a problem at a very young age, an explanation of when and how to address them is included. Throughout this section, I will refer to terms that were explained earlier in this book, like time-out, reinforcement, token systems, and so forth. Be sure to refer back to these sections if you are not sure how to enforce these techniques.

Successful parenting takes energy and a strong belief that what you are doing is right. It requires persisting with your approach of commitment, respect, trustworthiness, and good technique, even when you feel frustrated that it may not be "working." Remember that you are working for a long-term outcome, not applying a "quick fix" to your child's difficult behaviors. For more information about any of these situations, discuss your concerns with a physician or child psychologist.

Baby Brother or Sister

BRINGING A NEW BABY into the house is an exciting event for everyone, but an older brother or sister, especially a toddler, can easily feel displaced or jealous. You will want to do everything you can to insure that your child makes a smooth adjustment to this new family member, but how well you can prepare him or her for a new baby will depend on your child's stage of development. Before the Talker stage, a child will not understand that a baby is coming, and the concept will be vague even to a three-year-old. Several activities can help build your child's interest and excitement, and make the baby's arrival more real to him. Read books about babies, point out other children who have younger brothers or sisters, and take your child to sibling classes at the hospital where you plan to deliver.

Before the baby arrives, look for ways to get your child used to being away from you for short periods of time. Use a sitter now and then, or involve your child in a playgroup or preschool. Other adults and activities eventually may be more interesting than watching you take care of the baby, and helping your child feel comfortable spending some time away from you will help give you a break after the baby comes. If your child associates an abrupt change in time spent with you with the arrival of a new sibling, he may have negative feelings from the start.

Changes in your child's physical surroundings will tell him that someone else will soon be joining your household. Begin preparing the baby's room two or three months ahead of time and involve your child in the process. Put up the crib and talk about the new baby who will be sleeping in it. Move your child to a big bed only if you have several months to allow him to get used to his new furniture; otherwise borrow a crib and wait until things settle down afterward, so he doesn't feel that the baby is replacing him. Let your child stack diapers in the changing table or put toys in the baby's crib. If he wants to, let him draw a picture or pick out a toy for the baby, but be careful to explain that the baby won't be able to play with him right away.

Plan ahead to make your child feel important when the baby comes by letting him hold his new sibling soon after the birth. Point out the baby's fingers, toes, and other parts and talk about how much the baby can learn from your child. Remind your child that the baby is small and helpless and won't be able to do all the things you do with your child for several years.

Including your child in your baby's arrival will help him welcome his new brother or sister into the house. However, once the baby has been home awhile, it may be a different story. No matter how excited your child has been for months before, having a new sibling who cries and demands your attention may not be what he expected. Many children treat a new baby with curiosity at first and disinterest or jealousy once the novelty wears off. "When do we take the baby back?" is a question many children innocently ask about a new brother or sister.

CRAWLERS AND WALKERS

Crawlers are usually not very aware of a new baby; Walkers often are curious at first and overly zealous with hugs and kisses. At this age, your child is not likely to show outright jealousy, but she will probably notice a change in the amount of time you are able to spend with her and increase her demands for your attention. She may want to be held more than usual or cling to you when you try to leave. Punishing your child for her enthusiastic or needy behavior is not the answer. Supervise her whenever she is around the baby, distract her with toys, and attend to her whenever possible. Let her help you by handing you diapers or socks, and reinforce her whenever she plays appropriately near the baby.

TALKERS AND THREES

Threes, and sometimes Talkers, want to be big kids and help with a new baby, often treating her like a doll. They lift her too tightly, carry her roughly, and do not have good judgment about what is dangerous to an infant. *Don't leave your child alone with the baby.* Even though he may not mean to hurt his sibling, his jealousy may make him a little aggressive at this age so allow him to play with or hold the baby only with your supervision. Your child may also want to act like a baby again by trying on a diaper or drinking from a bottle. Let him regress just a little, as long it is done "just for pretend," but don't give in on big things like sleeping in your bed.

This is a time when children tend to test the limits because your attention is turned to other things. Don't slacken your basic rules because you feel sorry for your child. Offer some special toys or tasks he can do only when you are feeding the baby. Give him a way to help by holding the bottle or "reading" to the baby, or have him do what you are doing with his doll, rocking and feeding it perhaps. Be careful not to force him to do these things; they should be fun activities that make him feel important to you and show that he can benefit from the baby's presence. If he doesn't want to participate, just label his feelings for him: "I know you feel left out when I'm rocking the baby." Promise, "When I am done, I will play with (or rock) you." Then be sure to follow through. Consider getting a sitter for the baby once in a while so you can take your older child on a special outing. Tell him ahead of time so he can look forward to it, and remind him that this is your time together, just you and him.

Bedwetting

ALTHOUGH MOST CHILDREN stay dry at night by age three, bedwetting is not uncommon in children under five years of age. Even then, many children still wet the bed occasionally, and it is generally not considered a problem until age six or seven. Because a medical condition such as a urinary tract infection can sometimes be involved, it is always a good idea to consult with your doctor about your child's bedwetting. However, if there is no medical reason for the behavior, your child's bladder probably just needs to grow or his sphincter muscles to strengthen with further development. In the meantime, the following suggestions may help reduce the incidence of accidents.

- ◆ Give your child plenty to drink during the evening, but restrict fluids within an hour of bedtime.
- ◆ Have your child empty her bladder before going to bed, then waken her for a bathroom trip (or just carry her in and put her on the toilet) before you go to bed.
- ◆ Be pleased about dry nights, but don't shame, ridicule, or spank your child for wetting the bed. Simply change the sheets without drama or anger. Help siblings and other relatives understand how important it is to be supportive.

(continued)

◆ For a child age three or older, try using Pull-Ups or several pairs of underwear at once instead of diapers. Encourage your child to try to remain dry, but realize that she cannot voluntarily control her bladder at night. Say, "Tomorrow's another night. You can try again." Don't be surprised if your child's bedwetting is better *or* worse away from home, on a vacation or at grandparents' houses, due to changes in her sleep cycle when she is in unfamiliar territory.

◆ When your child is three or older, he might be helped by giving fluids during the day and challenging him to "hold it" for a period of time to stretch the bladder a little. But don't take this to an extreme and make him uncomfortable; there is a limit to the effectiveness of this procedure.

◆ Remember that none of these suggestions should take the place of the advice of your physician. Some manufacturers make a pad for the bed that sets off a bell when it is barely wet. This wakens some children in time to get to the bathroom. Your physician can tell you whether this type of device is appropriate for your child.

Biting

BABIES AND CRAWLERS

Babies are mostly toothless and do not bite intentionally. Putting things into their mouths is a way of exploring and learning about objects, not misbehaving. Teething increases the urge to gnaw on things, so give your Baby objects that are safe and appropriate to bite, such as teething toys or rubber rings that are made to be frozen and soothing to gums.

CRAWLERS AND WALKERS

When children bite other people during the Crawler or Walker stage, they aren't trying to hurt them, just practicing what comes naturally from curiosity or frustration. Biting is a way of acting on the environment that happens to produce interesting reactions from everyone around. Another child's arm or leg may simply be convenient when your child has the urge to attack something or to defend himself. That doesn't mean that biting should be allowed to continue. As soon as a bite occurs, tell your child, "No bite," and move him a few feet away. Withdraw your attention during a brief time-out. In the future, prevent the bite entirely, if possible, by redirecting your child whenever he looks as though he is about to bite. Remind him, "No bite," and praise him when he does something else that is appropriate.

TALKERS AND THREES

Because biting is a natural defensive behavior that usually arises out of frustration, your Talker or Three will probably bite someone at one time or another. Often, biting is the result of having an object taken away or not being allowed to do something. Your child may simply lash out at the most available person. How frequently your child bites may reflect her general frustration level, but she is most likely to do it under crowded conditions, in a noisy or chaotic environment, or when she is bored.

Although it may be tempting to "teach your child a lesson" by spanking her or biting her back, this is never a good idea. These behaviors hurt. It may seem as though they will teach her not to bite other people, but she is too young to think of things from another person's perspective, and understand that her behavior causes them pain. Even if she could empathize with them, she might not be able to resist biting again when her frustration gets high. If you spank your child for biting, she will learn to be aggressive. If you bite her, she will remember that you bite, too, and think it is acceptable; she won't learn alternative ways to express her frustration. Remember that successful parenting means being proud of the way you treat your child. Spanking or biting her probably don't qualify.

Try giving your child other things to chew on and keeping her occupied. Make sure the environment is not overly crowded and offers many activities to do and adults to interact with. If your child must stay in the setting in which she is biting, watch her carefully in order to prevent it. The only way to keep her from biting is to catch the behaviors that lead up to biting and use Progressive Discipline techniques when they occur.

If your child bites frequently, ask your spouse, an older child, or a babysitter to help supervise the other children your child is around, so you can watch your child closely for a day or two. Stay close to your child and notice which children she seems most agitated and frustrated around. Redirect her when she shows interest in taking another child's toy or becomes angry that someone took hers. When you are sure she is about to bite, respond immediately by saying "No bite!" sharply and clapping your hands to stop the bite quickly. Take away any reinforcement by immediately moving her a few feet away and ceasing interaction with her. Whether you use a time-out chair and how long you leave her there will depend on your child's developmental level, but wait a few moments before putting her back near the other children. When you do bring her back, remind her: "Don't bite." Call her attention to an acceptable toy or activity, and praise or reinforce her when she goes to it.

Redirection and time-out won't stop a child from biting after being done just a few times, but they will help reduce the behavior. Observe closely so you know what your child does just before he bites and which situations are likely to lead to trouble. Intervene in as many of these situations as you can, and you will make a significant impact on your child's biting behavior.

One last note: The child who is bitten should be attended to before the biter, especially if he is badly hurt. Make sure that you or someone else assists to the victim immediately, then deal as quickly as possible with the problem behavior.

Chores

HOW OLD MUST A CHILD be to actually contribute to the work of the household? Generally, much older than the ages discussed in this book. However, allowing your child to help with your chores can entertain him, and your patience with his early attempts will teach him that someday he will be expected to do these things, too. By the Walker stage, most children can follow simple commands and understand that they must put away what they pull out. However, a Walker's attention span is short, and he won't be able to work unsupervised. He won't be able to clear every toy off the floor or put every game piece back in its box without help, but he can learn to comply when you say, "Put the doll away now. It's time to eat dinner." Notice that I did not say, "Clean up your room." This command is too vague and means different things to different people. A young child will almost certainly misunderstand it. If you want your child to know what to do, you must be *specific* with your request, and it must be something he can finish quickly before he loses concentration.

Remember that to build successful experiences and encourage some semblance of the final behavior you want, you must reinforce your child's attempts as he goes along. Give him a simple, specific action you want him to do, like, "Put the doll in the box," and give him a few seconds to respond. Remember that a Walker or a Talker may not understand what you want him to do. If he doesn't do it, move closer to him and point to the doll and then the box, or move his arm gently in the direction of one, then the other. Physical prompts like this can help him understand and comply.

If your prompt does not succeed in getting your child to act, put your hand on his shoulder, look into his eyes and say his name with the request. "Robby, put the doll in the box." If he doesn't respond at this point, you will need to judge whether he doesn't understand the request, is too engrossed in what he is doing, or is just being stubborn. Be careful not to assume the latter too quickly. Some children take a few moments to process what they are asked to do. Say the command again and take his hand through the motion of picking up the doll and dropping it into the box. Thank him when you are done, even though he had little to do with the behavior. Then tell him to pick up the next object and wait for him to comply. The goal is to get success in response to at least one command. When your child is much older, you will be able to tell him to pick *all* the toys up off the floor, but for a Talker or a Three, one or two objects is probably enough to consider yourself successful at getting his compliance.

By the time a child is three, using a token reward system can encourage him to pick up toys or put his stuffed animals onto his bed on a regular basis. But don't expect him to do it spontaneously or all by himself. You will need to prompt and reward his efforts so he learns to comply with such requests.

Crying

BABIES AND CRAWLERS

It is easy to think that your Baby has figured you out because he stops crying when you comfort him, but don't fall into the trap of thinking he is crying on purpose. Your Baby doesn't do things to make you miserable or even to get you to come. He was simply born with a crying instinct that is useful to him; the most he can do is recognize a situation as familiar when it occurs. Letting your Baby cry a little while you figure out what the trouble is won't harm him, but responding to him at this age won't spoil him, either. Research has shown that Babies whose parents respond quickly to them cry less, not more, than those who are left to "cry it out." Responding consistently to his cries eventually will teach him that his behavior gets a response, which is an important aspect of learning. At this stage it will teach him that you are a reliable source of comfort.

Certain physical conditions such as colic and milk intolerance result in some infants being fussier than others. When you can't console your fussy Baby, you can easily think you are not a competent parent, but crying is biologically programmed to be distressing to adults. It is just a signal that some need is not being met. Stay objective while you figure it out. That on-edge feeling is a normal reaction to crying. While you are thinking of possible solutions to your baby's distress, try these suggestions:

- Rocking
- Cuddling
- Rhythmic movement
- Sound changes
- Visual changes in environment
- Swaddling

If none of these approaches works, put your child in a safe place and go outside for a moment, take a quick shower, or call a friend for support. Step back before you get too upset, and never, ever shake your Baby. Shaking a Baby can cause brain damage, blindness, and even death.

WALKERS, TALKERS, AND THREES

Excessive crying after the first year can be related to many things: physical illness, temperament, or noncompliance. Take your child to a physician to rule out any medical condition, then concentrate on your Progressive Discipline techniques. Remember that attention and positive reinforcement can increase compliance, and time-out is effective in decreasing inappropriate behaviors. For assistance in dealing with excessive crying, consult your physician or a child psychologist.

Day Care and Sitters

BABIES AND CRAWLERS

Babies and Crawlers can't tell you if they are happy at a new sitter's house or day-care center, but any child can object to a disruption in his routine. Babies may have difficulty sleeping or feeding at first, and older Crawlers may shrink from people with whom they are not familiar. In any of these new situations, give your child a few weeks to settle into the new routine. If possible, identify one or two people who will be providing most of his comforting, and transfer your child right into that person's arms. Send your child with an item or two he uses to comfort himself, like his pacifier, a sleep toy, or his blanket, but make sure your sitter or childcare worker knows how important these objects are to your child. If possible, purchase duplicates so you have a back-up if one of them is lost.

WALKERS, TALKERS, AND THREES

Your Walker, Talker, or Three may show his difficulty making the transition from home to a childcare center or sitter by crying when you leave or not wanting to go at all. Your child will be able to tell if you are feeling sad and anxious about leaving him and have even more anxiety about staying, so watch your mood on the way to the childcare setting. Do whatever you can to convey to your child that you see this as a positive place to be. When our children went through this stage, my husband and I referred to the day-care center as "school," since that sounded pretty grown up to our Talker. We told our daughter that our job was to go to work and her job was to go to school, because she had things to do, too. We told her that there is nothing for children to do at work, which helped her know that we weren't just abandoning her for a fun time she wasn't invited to share. We promised to pick her up as soon as work was over and to do something fun with her, even if that simply meant reading a book or holding her in a lap when we got home.

On the way to the center each day, I tried to have a positive attitude in the car. At the risk again of sounding like Mary Poppins (or Snow White, actually), I made up a song to use on our way to school, which I sang to the tune of a famous Disney song. I'd sing, "Hi ho. Hi ho, it's off to school we go. We work and play, have fun all day, Hi ho, Hi ho." Songs like this one helped my child think of the day-care center as a fun outing, not the dreaded start of another week.

Within a few blocks of the center, I played a little game with my child: "Can you find your day care?" I'd say. I'd point to a house or a gas station, and ask: "Is *that* your day care?"

"No," she'd say.

I'd find another house. "Is that your day care?"

"No!" she'd laugh.

Finally, I'd point to the actual day-care center. "Is *that* your day care?"

"Yes!" she'd say, excited that she had found it.

"Good for you!" I'd chime in. "You found your day care!"

This silly little game helped my daughter anticipate where she was going and look forward to finding it, rather than being apprehensive about its appearance. I acted glad to see it too, even when I secretly would rather have stayed home with her, too.

Once your child is inside the day-care center or sitter's house, getting yourself back out the door can be difficult. He may beg and plead, cling to you, follow you, or cry. These are unpleasant behaviors, especially when you wish you didn't have to leave your child, either. Slow your departure just a little and try to interest your child in an activity. If he resists the distraction or persists in following you and begging you to stay, try handing him directly to one of the day-care workers. Ask the worker to hold your child, or at least his hand, and engage him in an activity for a few minutes until you are out the door. Request this of the worker directly, by asking him or her to take your child to the block area or even to rock him for a few minutes. If the worker doesn't help, talk about it after your child has gone off to play, or later on the phone. Explain that you know the worker can't hold your child for long, but that it would help him make the transition. If the worker can't or won't oblige, speak to a supervisor or find a new day-care center. This is not a lot to ask.

When you are leaving your child at a day-care center or sitter's house, leave quickly, but never without saying goodbye. Sneaking off will create suspicion and make your child distrust you in the future. Use a short ritual (a hug, a kiss, high fives, etc.) if it helps to comfort your child and prepare him for your departure, but remember that your child will expect this

How you feel when leaving your child in day care or with a sitter will depend on your comfort with your childcare provider. Try the following suggestions to increase your confidence level:

1. Set reasonable expectations about how your child will be treated and share them with the day-care center or sitter.

2. Know what goes on there while you are gone:

   • Ask for a brief account of your child's day—either verbally or on paper. Use this basic information about when your child ate, slept, and had bowel movements to ask other questions you may tend to forget. Request to be told about any bumps or accidents your child has, no matter how minor.

   • Arrive unannounced at the center to watch how things are going. Only use a childcare setting that will allow you do this freely and unannounced.

   • For security reasons, be sure that there is a sign-out and identification process when children are picked up, and watch to be sure that it is being used.

   • Ask about discipline and other policies. If the methods or rules aren't exactly the same as in your home, you'll be more comfortable if you are sure the philosophy matches yours.

   • Ask about the policy on caring for a child who is not feeling well. At what point do they not want an ill child in the center? Under what conditions will you be expected to take your child home?

   • Do your research: Check with your state licensing agency or board to make sure the childcare center or sitter meets licensing requirements. Ask for names and phone numbers of other parents who have used the center and ask them about their experiences. If a center or sitter won't provide names of references, don't use that setting for childcare.

3. Have a backup plan for another sitter or day care in case you decide you aren't comfortable with something you have seen or heard.

every day and may be very distressed if you forget to do it. I once drove off without waving to my child and had to drive all the way back from work in order to keep my trust points! However, once you have finished your ritual and left the room, don't go back in, even if your child is crying—this will only reinforce his distress and tell him that you are feeling hesitant to leave. Watch him through an observation window or open door if you are sure you can do it without being seen, or call the center later to ask how your child is doing. Chances are, your child will stop crying within a few minutes of your departure and play happily with the other children.

If your child has a great deal of difficulty settling into a new environment, try leaving him for only a half-hour or so the first day before you go back to get him. If he is crying when you return, wait (where he can't see you) for a pause in his fussing, then go in and announce that it is time to go home. Gradually increase the amount of time you leave him at the center, but only for a day or two. After that, he should be fairly comfortable in his new surroundings. Whenever you come back for him, ask him to show you what he and the other children did while you were gone, visit with his friends for a few minutes, and talk about what they might do the next day when he returns. Your actions tell him that you like where he has been, he will be going back again, and he can depend on you to return for him.

Divorce

WHEN A DECISION IS MADE to end a marriage, many couples become concerned about the effect the changes will have on their children. Children often show anxious, angry, or regressive behaviors when they hear their parents argue and become confused and insecure when they separate. You can help your child adapt to this difficult situation by paying close attention to several issues:

1. Although very young children can't think about a rationale for the change in their family makeup, Talkers and Threes often want to know why it is happening. Some children believe that if they just hadn't misbehaved, their parents would stay together. Tell your child directly that the divorce is not his fault, but don't confuse him with a detailed explanation. Adult opinions and issues are inappropriate for young children to know about. Keep your explanation simple and without statements of blame, and make it clear that the divorce is not about your child.

2. Tell your child you love him even if you have told him many times before. He will need to hear it a lot at this time.

3. Give your child permission to love both parents. Say this explicitly and sincerely, including during some occasion when you and your spouse are together with your child.

4. Be very consistent and follow through with promises and discipline. Trust points are extremely important at this time.

5. Alone with your spouse, discuss your rules for your child's behavior. When possible and reasonable, support each other in any disciplinary actions you take. Try to agree on the basics, and don't argue about them later in front of your child. Talk about what calls for time-out and what behaviors need to change, and discuss any reward systems together. Conduct your discipline the same way in both households if possible, or explain matter-of-factly to your child what things you will be doing differently at your house.

(continued)

6. Talk with your spouse away from your child about plans, special events, visitation, and trips. Don't use your child to convey messages about these matters to your spouse.

7. Don't talk negatively about your spouse to your child. This will confuse and frighten your child and make him more likely to hide his own feelings.

8. Expect some regressive behaviors. Your child will need extra hugs and attention during this time, but be careful not to back off from your basic rules. Structure and consistency will help him feel secure while relationships and living arrangements are changing.

Eating Out

EATING IN RESTAURANTS or at friends' homes poses special challenges to parents: It means they must stay one step ahead of their child to insure that he doesn't start making his own entertainment. A child who screams or fusses can embarrass parents and convince them to let him do whatever he wants— or to not take him out again! However, the children who do best in public places are the ones whose parents insist on taking them along and focus their attention on helping them behave. If you don't want to leave your child home while you go out, you must keep him entertained, and depending on your child's temperament, your early experiences may not be entirely pleasant. Explain to the people who go out with you that you can't give them your full attention when you are teaching your child to behave.

When entertaining your child in a restaurant, don't overlook the usual objects you have with you or those you find along the way. Something that is common to you may be a novel and entertaining toy to your child. Be mindful of safety issues and don't give your child something that is dirty or has sharp edges or small pieces (under two inches in diameter) that can be swallowed if they come off. Here is a list of "found objects" your children may find particularly interesting. Remember, providing these items is no substitute for supervision. You will still need to guide their use.

- Photographs or ID cards
- Gloves
- Plastic or paper cups
- Rinsed film canisters (without very small lids) with cereal inside
- Keys
- Magazines
- Cellular phones without batteries
- Hairbrushes or combs
- Spoons
- Paper (even the deposit slip from your checkbook)
- Sticky note pads
- Pencils and pens

BABIES

Because Babies sleep a lot, they are usually easy to take to restaurants. However, this can mean planning around naps and being willing to feed your child during your meal. Children with colic or other uncomfortable physical conditions require rocking, walking, and understanding. A Baby will find a new environment entertaining for only a brief period of time; don't expect him to behave differently in public than he does at home.

CRAWLERS AND WALKERS

Some Crawlers and Walkers become easily bored; others seem to entertain themselves. All of them have their limits. Don't expect your child to be a little adult and sit through a leisurely dinner without protest, no matter how much you have been looking forward to going out. It is not his fault that he wants to explore the world. At this age, plan to entertain him or stay home.

When you take your Crawler or Walker to a restaurant, pick a family-oriented place where you can be served quickly, and take things along for your child to play with. Much like a treasure drawer at home, a bag of forgotten trinkets and a few basic items like markers, paper, blocks, and rattles can provide many minutes of entertainment for a child. Take crackers, a bag of cereal, or whatever you can present as a surprise to keep him occupied and ward off hunger while you wait for your meal. Don't always carry the same things, and don't show them to your child before you go; just present them when he begins to get restless.

Transitional objects like pacifiers, blankets, or a favorite stuffed animal can help a tired or fussy child get through an evening out. Choose a pacifier that can be found easily in any drugstore or grocery store in case it is lost. Consider pinning the stuffed animal or blanket to your child's clothing or attaching a short, loose elastic band to secure his pacifier to his wrist. Never attach a cord longer than three to four inches as it can create a strangulation hazard.

THREES

By age three, children can be expected to stay occupied for brief periods of time without being heavily entertained. Still, it is a good idea to have your child practice sitting still at home before you go to a restaurant, counting out loud how long he can do it and reinforcing success. When you go out, take along a favorite toy, book, or pad of paper and pencil to keep him interested in an activity. Refresh his interest frequently by reading a page of his book, drawing a face for him to complete, or giving him something to draw, and be sure to tell him what a nice job he is doing when he plays on his own with his toys. At the table or on the way home, tell your friends how pleased you are with your child's behavior.

Exploring Body Parts

AT ANY AGE, it is common for children to touch their genitalia, and this is of concern only if it is done excessively or in public. Young children explore this part of their body with the same curiosity they do their face or feet, without regard for social expectations or propriety. Sometimes they discover that touching can be pleasurable, which is also natural and not something to punish. If your child touches his or her genital area frequently around others, supervise him or her so you will know when it is most likely to happen, and do not overreact when it occurs. Treat touching "private parts" the same way you would any other undesired behavior, matter-of-factly and without shaming. Give your child an alternative behavior or redirect him to a more private place. Tell him (in a whisper if others are present), "You need to go to your room or the bathroom if you want to touch yourself there."

When your child shows curiosity about his or her body, use accurate names for the parts he points out, including penis and vagina. Giving your child a vocabulary for discussing these parts can make it easier to talk about his body. Teach him that, other than him, only his parents or a doctor should ever touch these parts of his body, and as soon as he is able, let him take care of washing himself. Tell him that no one should make him feel uncomfortable about his body, and to talk to you if they do.

Occasionally, there can be medical reasons for a child touching his or her genital area, like diaper rash or an infection. Check with your doctor if you think this is a possibility, or if you believe your child could be imitating inappropriate touching he has seen or experienced.

Fears

BABIES AND CRAWLERS

Because Babies don't yet recognize anything as threatening, they are not usually fearful, but by the late Crawler stage, children become highly aware that their parents and other adults are not the same people. Your Crawler may smile and wave happily at others from the safety of your arms but shy away or cry when she is approached. At this stage, she will be highly aware as you get ready to leave the room and cry or search anxiously for you when you disappear from view. For brief absences, you may be able to calm your child by talking to her when you are in nearby rooms. When you must leave your child with another caretaker for longer times, your child's distress about your departure is unlikely to last more than a few minutes. Remember that this change means your child has developed new memory skills. She will soon realize that you return when you leave her, and your departure will not be as distressing.

WALKERS, TALKERS, AND THREES

Walkers and Talkers often fear common things like toilets flushing or a vacuum cleaner running. Thunder and lightning, dogs and cats, and other things that move or make noise can cause a child in these stages to squeal with panic. Young children also have trouble knowing what is real and what is not, especially if they have had their imagination triggered by a story or the television. By three, many children are fearful if their room is too dark.

Your response to your child's behavior is important in insuring that his fears do not become ingrained. Punishing your child's fear or joking about it can make him feel shamed and even more fearful. If the feared situation is one you can't avoid, like going to the doctor or walking past a dog, offer comfort and sympathy, but not too much. Insist confidently, without anger or annoyance, that the activity is necessary. Remember that you are modeling how to respond to the feared object or situation, and be calm and self-assured even if the situation also is uncomfortable to you. Here are some important points to remember:

- Your child's fears are real to him. Recognize his concern by saying, "I understand that you are afraid." Then tell him why that isn't necessary: The feared object can't harm him, is tied up, is far away, or simply that you will protect him.

- Show your child that you are not afraid (or can deal with your fear) by being calm in the situation. Talk as positively as possible about the thing he fears, like, "Look at this little spider. We must look huge to him!" (Obviously, stay clear of black widows, brown recluse spiders, or other things that actually are dangerous.) If you are fearful, tell him as calmly as possible that you are going to seek assistance, and move him gently away.

- Talk about the "good" things the feared thing does, like rain growing gardens, spiders helping plants stay healthy, or medicine keeping people from getting sick.

- Allow your child to observe others dealing with the feared object or situation, or show pictures and movies about it.

- Use distraction techniques to take his mind off the situation: Read a story, talk about other more pleasant events, blow a pinwheel, bat a balloon, or tell him to close his eyes and picture something pretty.

- Find a smaller example of the feared thing for your child to get used to, like a stuffed animal or a puppy instead of a full-grown dog.

- Role-play a situation in which your child, or you, must be brave about a feared object or situation. Allow your child to be the doctor and give you a shot, or the letter carrier who tames a growling dog.

- Approach the feared situation together, holding hands or carrying your child, if necessary. Then gently encourage him to "try it himself."

- Play with something your child really likes only when the feared situation is present, such as reading a special book when it thunders or playing with cards while you sit at the doctor's office.

- Quickly finish any unpleasant but necessary event like an immunization shot. Tell your child it will be over soon, count to three with (or for) him, and do it. Comfort and praise him when it is over.

Remember that your child is going to sense and imitate how you act in a feared situation. Try not to get angry with him or worry for him. If you are too anxious to demonstrate that there is nothing to fear, your efforts to calm him will not be reassuring. In fact, they may make him even more anxious. If you have persistently tried several of these approaches, and your child's fear is interfering with some part of his life, discuss your concerns with a child psychologist or your physician.

Getting Ready to Go Somewhere

BABIES AND CRAWLERS

Babies and Crawlers are generally easy to move from one activity to another; however, parents who do this too abruptly can cause their child to resist preparations like putting on coat or mittens, or to cry unnecessarily. Talk calmly to your child as you quickly dress her for the out-of-doors. Let her hold a rattle or mirror, or distract her by making silly noises and faces as you work.

WALKERS, TALKERS, AND THREES

Helping your Walker, Talker, or Three make a transition from one activity to another can be difficult, especially if you are in a hurry. No matter how far ahead you plan, your child may refuse to come when you call him. "Hurry up," you might say. "I'm going to be late."

She looks at you and keeps playing with her toys.

"Now," you say. "Get your coat on."

She cries and refuses to put her arm in the sleeve. Why should she put on a coat when she can do so many other things, like dig through her toy box, chase the dog, or run away from you?

Perhaps you are making too abrupt a transition. You may have forgotten to view the situation through your child's eyes and to make the next activity seem interesting and worth doing. Try kneeling or crouching down at eye-level with your child and commenting on his or her activity: "Bowser likes to chase the ball when you throw it, doesn't he?" Call her attention to the next thing you are going to do: "I can't wait to see Grandma, how about you?" or "I want to sing that 'Riding in the Car' song this morning. I wonder what we'll see out the window?"

If that doesn't entice your child to cooperate, the next step is to make what your child wants to continue doing, like throwing Bowser's ball, contingent on making a move toward the door. Allow her to throw it a couple of times, then promise she can do it one more time, but add, "Get your coat on first." The promise of something she wants to do will encourage her to move toward your goal. Help her to start thinking about what is going to happen next: "Let's play that new song when we get in the car, okay?" If she insists on continuing the game after she does it one last time, set the ball on the counter and tell her, "We'll throw this again for Bowser when we get home. Right now, we need to get to Grandma's house." Add a choice of behaviors at that point, just to give her some control in the situation: "Do you want to take your doll or your crayons with you in the car?" She may choose to take both, and that's okay, as long as she heads for the door.

If your child simply does not want to cooperate when you have made the next step as enticing as possible, use time-out or simply carry her to the car. If your child is Three or older, and getting ready to go somewhere is a frequent problem, consider challenging her in the future with a token reward system. Use a timer and let her know how quickly she must be ready in order to earn her tokens.

Here are some suggestions to help get your child out the door:

- Let her know a few minutes ahead of time that it is almost time to go.

- Show interest in her current activity by getting down at her level and commenting, sports-caster-like, about what she is doing.

- Find something of interest to her that you can make contingent on her getting her arm in the sleeve or her shoes on her feet.

- Suggest she take a favored object with her to help her make the transition.

- Make it fun by suggesting you "race" to the door to get coats on; or that you beat the timer, do it before the music box stops, etc.

- If all else fails, tell her to put her coat on or you'll "help" her do it; then put one of her arms in the sleeve and say, "Thank you. Now put your other arm in." If she resists, simply do it for her. This is an opportunity to guide her to learn the appropriate, desired behavior. Thank her for doing what you actually made her do so she will remember the physical motions she went through in order to receive your praise.

- With a child who is being deliberately difficult, use time-out only if you are sure he understood what you were asking him to do. Start earlier next time so you can afford to wait for him to comply, and he can't avoid time-out just because you are in a hurry to get somewhere.

- When you are in too much of a hurry to effectively use time-out or other techniques, avoid the struggle. Carry her in one arm, her shoes in the other, and take her calmly to the car.

Getting Your Child to Sleep

GETTING YOUR CHILD TO SLEEP can be one of the biggest frustrations known to parents. Not getting enough sleep yourself is often the result. From very early on the struggle to get your child to sleep can affect your child's behavior, your family's functioning, and how you feel about your child. For infants and babies, not sleeping usually means crying and fussing whenever you lay them in bed or leave the room; for older children it can involve getting out of bed, coming to find you, complaining of stomach aches, fearing monsters, and requesting drinks, bathroom breaks, backrubs, etc. These demanding behaviors can go on for hours and are enough to wear any parent to a frazzle. You are all undoubtedly tired. You must help him learn to comfort himself to sleep.

Obviously, you can't make your child go to sleep; you can only reinforce behaviors that help him get to sleep, like staying in his room, staying in bed, and lying quietly in semidarkness. Your first task is to get him into bed. Establish a bedtime routine that begins about thirty minutes before you hope to leave your child's room to signal what is coming and give him a chance to wind down and relax. Depending on your child's age, his bedtime routine might include brushing his teeth, going to the toilet, reading, and cuddling. Give him cues that sleep time is coming, such as low light, quiet voices, slowed activity, a sleep toy, a favorite song, or a backrub, but don't make your list too long. Even before he is old enough to say the words, your child will remind you firmly of any steps you leave out.

Parents often make the mistake of putting their child to bed after he has fallen asleep elsewhere. Rocking him until he is completely asleep or letting him fall asleep on the couch may seem convenient and harmless, but these behaviors can spell trouble. Doing them even occasionally can lead a child to expect and demand such treatment. Remember that behaviors that are occasionally reinforced can be more difficult to extinguish later. If your child doesn't learn to comfort himself and fall asleep on his own, bedtime—and the rest of the night—can be very difficult.

Like adults, children partially waken on their own several times per night. Usually, they look around, adjust their position, and go quietly back to sleep. However, when children wake to find that they are no longer in their parents' arms or on the cozy couch with the television on, they are likely to bolt awake, cry, and demand to be comforted back to sleep. Needing special conditions in order to sleep creates very real problems for you and your child.

BABIES

Under two months of age, Babies cry two or three times per night because they are hungry, but by three months of age, this behavior usually drops to once per night. A Baby can usually drift off to sleep after being comforted and laid in his crib. (The American Academy of Pediatrics recommends that Babies sleep on their backs until at least 6 months of age.) Rub or pat his tummy, arm, or leg for a minute or so and leave the room, but don't expect sleep always to happen immediately. The change in warmth or motion may cause him to cry briefly or he may just be over-stimulated by the day's events. Research has shown that babies who are responded to quickly and consistently cry less in later months than those left to "cry it out," but this doesn't mean you must respond immediately. Give him a chance to comfort himself. If he doesn't stop fussing after several minutes, he is probably uncomfortable in some way, either from external or internal sources. Crying at this age is not done intentionally to get your attention or make you mad. Your Baby can't plan ahead for you to come when he cries; he is simply preprogrammed to cry when he is uncomfortable. If he doesn't settle on his own, don't worry that you will spoil him. When he is this young, don't hesitate to respond.

If your child continues to fuss, check to see if he is wet or cold. Is there a pin poking him? Is there a string from his pajamas caught on his toe? If it has been at least two or three hours since his last feeding, go ahead and feed him to soothe and comfort him. Beyond these obvious problems, consider whether some internal discomfort, ache, or pain may be causing his distress. An illness or earache may require a trip to your doctor, or it is possible that he has colic. Colicky babies can arch their backs as though they have a tummy ache and cry continuously for hours. No one knows exactly what causes colic, but some doctors suspect a milk allergy, allergy to the environment, or swallowing air during feeding. Whatever its cause, colic can be very frustrating for parents, particularly in the evening or at bedtime when they are least emotionally equipped to deal with it. In most cases, colic just has to run its course, but ask your physician whether a special formula will help.

When your Baby can't get to sleep and continues to cry, try some of these suggestions:

1. If he needs to suck, offer a pacifier if necessary, but never put a bottle in the crib with him. Milk and juice can damage teeth, and any liquid creates a risk of choking.

2. Change his environment a little. Walk outside with him, play music, push him in a stroller.

3. Hold him closely or swaddle him in a blanket so his arms and legs don't flail freely.

(continued)

---

4. Walk with him in a baby carrier or sling, or rock him rhythmically back and forth. Try putting him up to your shoulder (facing over your shoulder) and bouncing rhythmically, once per second.

5. Lay him on his tummy across your knees and rub his back.

6. Arrange to have "white noise" droning in the background to block out household noises and soothe your Baby. Some stores sell white noise generators, but many household objects also produce this kind of noise: A fan, humidifier, or vacuum cleaner placed safely in the background where your child cannot be harmed by it can help lull him to sleep. Some manufacturers also make devices that simulate a heartbeat or vibrate the crib to help the Baby to sleep.

7. Put your child in a safe spot and step back before you get too upset. And *never, ever shake your Baby.* Shaking can cause brain damage, blindness, and even death.

8. Call a friend to help you cope, or phone the hospital nursery, a help line, or your physician to get suggestions for your Baby's care.

CRAWLERS AND WALKERS

As with Babies, Crawlers and Walkers need a bedtime routine, a few minutes of calming activities such as rocking, reading, snuggling, or looking at pictures; but try to avoid running through a long series of activities. One parent I know drove her child in the car every night; another played most of a John Denver tape. Taking extra steps or using lengthy routines to comfort your child to sleep can condition her to need these special activities.

Crawlers and Walkers usually stay in their cribs when put there, but be sure to put the side rails all the way up to insure that yours can't climb out. If she can, be concerned about her safety and follow the recommendations given in the next section on Talkers. If she can't climb out, lay her in her bed, pat her tummy or stroke her arm for a few moments, and use just a few words to signal that you will be leaving the room: "Good night, Cassie. See you in the morning." Then leave the room and shut the door at least most of the way. She may cry at first, but let her fuss for a few minutes. Although she may realize that you come to her rescue when she cries, this is still an unconscious connection. She isn't sitting in her crib plotting this out. She isn't truly afraid, either. She may be mad about your absence, but at this age, she can't think about any awful things that could happen if you aren't there to protect her.

If your child doesn't settle after five minutes, go back into the room and lay her down again. Pat her tummy or stroke her arm again for about fifteen seconds and say the same few words you said before: "Good night, Cassie. I'll see you in the morning," then leave again. Repeat this sequence five minutes later if your child is still crying. The next time, wait ten minutes before going back into the room, and after that, go in every fifteen minutes if she is crying when the time has elapsed.

Try not to give your Walker a bottle in the middle of the night. She doesn't really need one, and this will only condition her to demand a bottle in order to go back to sleep. Night feedings will cause her to urinate and possibly waken later. Keep trying to reduce the amount of food you give her during the night, and lengthen the intervals between feedings. When you are done with a feeding, pat her back and leave the room. If she fusses, and you feel guilty or sad, remember that you are helping her learn to comfort herself by letting her cry before she goes to sleep. If this is difficult because you need sleep and you think you will be tempted to go into her room to rescue her, start the training at naptime when you are better able to cope. Giving in once you start will make it more difficult for your Walker to learn to comfort himself and reduce the chances that this training process will work when you decide to try again.

TALKERS

Your Talker may not want to be left in her room at night because she has developed new memory skills that remind her that you are still available once you leave her room. She may even develop separation anxiety and put up a great fuss. If your Talker has difficulty going to sleep on her own but still stays safely in her crib, use the method described in the previous section to help her learn to comfort herself. Ideally, don't make the transition to a "big bed" until she learns to go to sleep on her own. However, if she can already climb out of her crib and you are concerned about her safety, move her to a bed.

If your child will not go to sleep in her new bed, her sleep problem will require a different approach. Your first task will be to get her to stay in her bed. This is where some of the behavioral techniques discussed earlier in the book will come in handy. Say, "Good night, Sarah, I'll see you in the morning." Then leave the room. If she stays in her bed and goes to sleep let her know how proud you are of her in the morning. If she repeatedly gets out of bed, keep putting her back. She cannot go to sleep while she is walking about the house, so tell her she must stay in her bed even if she can't sleep. Don't be tempted to let her fall asleep on the couch or in your room, either. This will not help her learn to sleep in her bed.

Some children have a great deal of difficulty learning to stay in bed because they are curious about what is happening in the rest of the house. Other children are anxious or have learned bad habits. Whatever the reason, these children will need extra help before they will go to sleep in their own bed. If your child is able to understand a promise of future behavior, say: "I'll be right back, Sarah. If you are in bed when I come back, I'll rub your back." Walk out of the room, count to twenty, and go back in to rub her back for about thirty seconds. Then say the same thing again: "Good night, Sarah. I'll be back in a few minutes to rub your back, but only if you are in bed." If she is not in bed when you return, put her there, saying: "I'm sorry, you got out of bed. No backrub this time. I'll be back in a few minutes to rub your back, but only if you're in bed."

Keep repeating this process, slightly lengthening how long you are gone each time. If you are consistent and show your child that you will follow through with your promise, you will succeed in teaching her to stay in bed. This means that even if she is almost asleep, you must still go back in her room and rub her back. This may seem counterproductive, but is an important part of earning trust points. It tells her that she can relax when you leave the room because you definitely will be back, even if she happens to go to sleep. In the morning, remind her that you did what you said you would do. Make a point of telling her that she was sound asleep the last time you came into her room, but you rubbed her back anyway. Be sure to tell her that you are proud of her for staying in her bed. After a few nights of this, your child is likely to stay in bed, relax, and fall asleep easier and faster than before.

Next, work on gradually lengthening the time you wait after leaving her room before you go back, to phase out her dependence on your coming into her room.

Most children respond well to this reinforcement technique, but sometimes a child's behavior gets out of hand. Occasionally, a child will need more distinct consequences for getting out of bed. My two-year-old was one of these very active children. She would not stay in bed unless I sat right there practically lying on top of her to keep her still, and she was out of bed as soon as I hit the door. As much as I hated it, I ended up telling her that I would take her pacifier if she got out of bed (a form of time-out that didn't require removing her from her bed, on which I wanted her to lie down and go to sleep!). I would not have used this technique before my child was two because she would not have understood my request. I also did not do it as punishment. It was time-out, time away from the reinforcement of her pacifier or my attention, and it lasted only a few seconds. That was all it took to make my point and teach her to stay in bed. The impact of the "time-out" procedure happened the moment I took the pacifier away from her. When she got out of bed, I told her, "You didn't stay in bed, so now I am taking your pacifier." I walked out of the room, counted to ten, then returned the pacifier to her immediately, saying, "Now stay in bed or I will take it again." I added gently, "I'll be back in a minute to rub your back, but you have to be in bed." I wanted to give her a chance to do it right the next time, and I wanted her to know she was back at square one again with me. Whenever I came back after that, she was waiting patiently in bed, and I rewarded her with a brief backrub. Eventually, she learned to fall asleep on her own.

THREES

The Threes stage can be even more difficult than the earlier years because children tend to want to delay sleep by asking many questions like, "Why do I have to go to bed?" and "What if there is something in the closet?" Be careful not to get caught in lengthy conversation. Give quick, concise answers to your child's questions and leave the room. Offer to rub her back if she is in bed when you return, or set up a token reward system, and give her a token each time you find her in bed. Since she might worry that she will miss her chance for a token if she goes to sleep before you come back, tell her that when you return, you will give her one token if she is in bed and two if she happens to be asleep. Discuss this again in the morning, and show her where you left the tokens the last time you visited her room. Be sure her tokens are exchangeable for something she can earn quickly, perhaps with only one night's earnings. Reinforce her soon after she has earned the required amount.

Although a simple reward system works well for most children, other children tend to be worriers. They get so fearful about being alone that they have a hard time learning to comfort themselves and will not stay in bed for a moment any time their parent leaves the room. Children this age often have difficulty knowing what is real and what is not. Try using a soft night-light, leaving the door open, and rewarding him for staying in bed for brief periods while you are out of the room. If he comes to you frantic that there is a monster in his room, be a little sympathetic and give him a quick hug on the way back to his room. Ask what he is scared of, reassure him that his fears are unfounded and that you will keep him safe, and show him that there is nothing scary in the place where he thought the monster might be. Then change the subject. Say, "Here's something different to think about: Think about our friends coming tomorrow or the time we went to the zoo." (Be careful not to pick a topic that will get him too excited. Anticipation can make it *harder* to go to sleep.) Get him talking briefly about the topic, but don't carry on a long conversation. Tell him you'll discuss it more in the morning, and leave the room. The goal is to get him to lie there on his own and go to sleep.

Remember that your child will sense and imitate your feelings in these situations. Try not to get angry at the inconvenience of reassuring him one more time or he may be angry in return. Try not to appear worried, either. If you are too anxious to demonstrate that there is no monster in the room by checking the closet, showing him the windows won't open, and assuring him the burglar alarm is on, you will plant ideas he hasn't even thought of yet. Unless he brings these things up, don't mention them; they may make the situation worse.

If, even after a bedtime routine, your child is so fearful that he cannot be convinced to stay in his room alone, you will have to brace yourself for a few nights of "training." Tell him you will sit by his door to read your book (to yourself), as long as he is in bed. Then stay there. Don't sneak off when he shuts his eyes. Wait until long after you are certain he is asleep or he will be popping up and down wondering when you are going to do it again. Resist the urge to lie down with him if he asks, or he will want you to do this every night. The goal of sitting nearby is to help him relax and experience falling asleep on his own, in his own bed. If he gets out of bed, tell him you will leave the room and shut the door if he does it again, then do it very briefly if that happens. You will want him to know you really mean it, but you won't want him to become frantic, so shut the door for only fifteen seconds. When you come back, put him into bed and go back to looking very engrossed in your reading. Repeat the sequence any time he gets up. Once he has experienced staying in bed and realizes you are going to stay right there, he will eventually fall asleep.

Over the next few nights, move your chair further from his bed until you are doing your reading in the hallway. Give him praise (or perhaps tokens) each morning if he has stayed in bed. As you move your chair further out the door, keep talking about what a "big kid" he is now that he has learned to go to sleep on his own. Finally, after a few nights of success, tell him you are not going to sit there tonight because you have other things to do, but promise that you will be back in a few minutes to check on him. Then leave the room entirely. Return in just a minute or two and reward him with a wave from the door, or, if necessary, a brief pat on the back, and repeat your promise that you will be back in another few minutes.

Increasing Compliance

"HE JUST DOESN'T LISTEN to me," I hear many parents say. "I tell him over and over to do something, and he acts like he doesn't hear me." This situation is frustrating but is not always a case of a child actively ignoring what you are saying. Poor listening often occurs when a child is intensely involved in an activity. His increasing concentration skills allow him to tune out whatever is going on around him, and this can look like naughtiness.

Before you treat your child as though he has misbehaved, be sure that he understands what you are asking him to do. The chart on page 196 shows what a child is likely to understand at different stages of development. Noncompliance can sometimes be a sign of hearing loss. Let your physician know if your child seems to be behind others his age in making speech sounds or if he says, "What?" a lot. Even when you are certain your child has heard you, remember that when they are young, children learn through repetition, not reasoning. Respond with patience and persistence. Give your child a consequence for noncompliance, but give it without anger. He must be shown over and over again how to comply.

Try the following steps to help your child comply with your requests:

◆ Say his name and wait until he looks at you to begin telling him your request.

◆ Be specific. Don't say, "Get ready to go," but rather, "Please put your coat on." Say it firmly, but in a friendly way.

◆ Tell what will be happening next to arouse his interest. Say kindly, "Please get your pajamas on so we can read your book."

◆ Word your requests as statements, not questions. The obvious answer to "Will you pick up your toy?" is "No."

◆ Give one instruction at a time and allow a few seconds for him to respond.

◆ If he doesn't respond, touch him lightly on the shoulder to prompt him.

◆ Wait until he's done responding to your request before making another one.

◆ Reward any effort to comply with your request, however small the approximation.

Commands Understood at Different Stages	
Stage	**Commands**
Baby (0–6 months)	• Follows no commands.
Crawler (6–12 months)	• Responds to changes in voice tone (cries at unpleasant or angry voice). • Responds to simple gestures and commands, like "Look" or "Patty Cake." • Doesn't stop at "No."
Walker (12–24 months)	• Usually follows simple command like "Give it to me." • Stops at words like "No" or "Hot."
Talker (24–36 months)	• Understands simple commands. • Follows simple directions, like "Put it back" or "Bring it here."
Three (36–48 months)	• Can do some two-step requests, like "Take this into the kitchen and put it on the counter." • Can do requested tasks that take a few minutes to finish. • Can't reason about rules. Can repeat them but may not think about them when appropriate in new situations. Rules must be repeated in context.

Increasing Independence

YOUR CHILD'S ABILITY to do things for himself will depend, of course, on his developmental level. As a Baby, he will be completely helpless; as a Crawler, his personal skills will be limited to drinking from a cup that is held for him or extending his arm to assist in dressing. By the time your child is a Talker, however, he will begin to show interest in doing things by himself, and possibly even in helping you. Doing too much for him can make him dependent and immature, but expecting him to do things he is not capable of remembering or physically carrying out will do him an even greater disservice over time. Allow your child to assist you, but realize that you won't actually get much (if any) real help. The important result of his efforts is that he believes he has helped you; it doesn't matter if things aren't done the way you or I would do them. Watch what your child tries to do on his own so that you have some idea how capable he is, then give him tasks you know he can accomplish. Realize that he will repeat his behaviors over and over again before he does them well, and try not to interfere with his practice. Having a sense of humor will help as you watch him practice taking his shoes off over and over again, often in inconvenient places.

If your child wants to do something himself but has difficulty with the task, let him do as much as he can, and then finish it for him. The easiest part of the task may be at the end, like putting the top piece of bread on a sandwich or pulling up the tops of his socks. Tell him that he will get to do the last step as soon as you're done with the first part, and let him finish the task. Praising his efforts will encourage him to keep trying. This, along with your guidance and reinforcement, will motivate him to learn and improve his self-concept.

Typical Self-Help Skills	
Baby (0–6 months)	• None • Later, holds bottle
Crawler (6–12 months)	• Holds out arm for sleeves and feet for shoes • Drinks from glass held by other
Walker (12–24 months)	• Takes off shoes or socks without help • Drinks from cup without help • Uses spoon
Talker (24–36 months)	• Dries hands • Uses fork, spoon, and cup • Pulls pants down • Later, puts on coat, not buttoning
Three (36–48 months)	• Takes care of bathroom needs (undresses, wipes, dresses) • Washes face and hands • Later, dresses completely except tying shoes

Lying

TALKERS AND THREES

Lying is a complex behavior. Technically, it involves deceiving someone and knowing that it is morally wrong. Most children under four years of age don't understand these concepts. They are often impulsive and take things that aren't theirs just because they want them. Young children break objects while exploring how they work or when they are overly rambunctious. Often, they can't think about the probable outcome of their behavior. Children under four can easily deny doing something they have just done.

I once watched a three-year-old take every penny out of a jar in his kitchen. He sat on the floor next to the empty jar with the pennies in his hand. When asked, he told his mother he didn't take them. She was understandably distressed that her child would "lie" so openly, but I reminded her that, at this age, children often do not differentiate between fantasy and reality. He could easily believe he hadn't taken them. Young children also tend to say what they think will please adults. When a child knows that whatever he has done has angered his parents, he may try to keep from upsetting them further by saying that he didn't do it. This is his way of saying, "I wish this hadn't happened."

The best way to help your child develop the concept of responsibility is to continually and calmly point out the connection between what he does and the outcome of his behavior. Say, "You leaned on your toy and broke it," or, "You took these pennies, and they belong to Daddy." If possible, give him a simple way to "make things right" so he can participate in fixing the problem and be back at square one again with you. Let him help you clean things up or suggest that he gather the pennies and give them back to Daddy.

Here are suggestions for teaching your child as much as he can grasp about the difference between telling the truth and lying:

◆ Talk about what is real and what is not; what *can* be true and what *can't*, on television, in books, and in life. *(continued)*

◆ Be careful to model trustworthiness. If you are deceptive or deny things you have done or said, you child will learn to do this too.

◆ When you catch your child taking something that isn't his, calmly tell him, "That belongs to ___. It isn't yours. Let's put it back." Make a very obvious effort to help your child return the things he takes and make a big deal out of needing to find their rightful owner. Your goal is to teach your child what is his and what isn't, and to state the truth: "I believe that you took the pennies from my jar." If you saw him do it, let him know what you saw. Don't ask if he did it and then have to deal with his lying as well. If he denies his actions, say what you *think* happened: "I believe you dropped this on the floor and broke it."

◆ Some older three-year-olds do begin to develop the idea of responsibility and deception and can actually tell a lie. However, it is best not to assume this unless you are sure. When in doubt, deal only with the broken rule, not the act of lying. If he knows what he did was wrong, put him in time-out briefly for his behavior, but don't punish him harshly; he may feel it is worth lying the next time to stay out of trouble.

Mealtimes

MEALTIME CAN BE THE CALMEST, happiest, most "family" time of the day, but not always with a young child in the house. Children don't sit still very long, even with food in front of them: They demand treats, refuse foods others prepare, and don't go very long without attention from parents. However, the goal of having a meal together goes beyond trying to get food into your child. Over time, eating together teaches your child a routine, underscores the importance of family, and establishes behaviors that will allow you to take him to restaurants or friends' houses with relative ease. Of course it helps if he is hungry, so be sure he hasn't been snacking all afternoon. Interact with him frequently—both you and food are powerful reinforcers that can be used to teach your child to cooperate.

Remember that no matter what you do, you are not likely to get your child to sit through a five-course meal or to eat all of his food. You must judge when to let him leave the table based on his behavior and his nutritional needs. When you want him to stay at the table, and he doesn't want to be there, give him the impression of control by offering simple choices, like whether he wants his sandwich cut in two pieces or four. If he decides that whatever he asked for is not what he wanted after all, distract him by moving on to some related topic of interest. "Hey, shall we put an olive on top? Let's make it into a face!"

Remember that you and your spouse may want to linger over coffee, but your child may barely get through the main course before wanting to get down. If your child refuses to eat, and this is unusual behavior for him, don't push it. He may be coming down with a cold or not be hungry. But if your child is well and refuses to sit calmly at a meal, he is probably just objecting to being confined to his chair. When you think he has eaten a reasonable amount and your distraction techniques are losing their effectiveness, excuse him from the table, but don't be tempted to let him come back to nibble whenever he pleases. When dinner is over, it should be over.

For a Walker, Talker, or Three, give a simple, easy request before you let him down so you can reward his *compliance* rather than his *fussing*. Set up a contingency: "You can get down after you eat one more bite," or, "Wipe your mouth and you can get down." Be sure to choose a request he is likely to follow, otherwise you may have to give in to misbehavior or reinforce the wrong thing, like struggling to get out of his chair or fussing and crying. If he is calm, reinforce any positive behavior you can as you let him go: "I like the way you ate all your beans," or, "You're such a big boy to sit at the table with us for so long." Use this as a chance to tell him exactly what you liked about his *recent* behavior, and you will increase the chance that he will repeat it the next time.

If your Walker, Talker, or Three is continually difficult at mealtimes, refuses to eat, or leaves the table whenever he pleases, find a highchair he can't climb out of and begin to train him to eat dinner with you. Put something tasty in front of him. If he pushes it away, tell him, "No, it is time to eat." Give the dish back to him, redirecting his attention to something about the food or the plate: "Do you see cheese in your sandwich?" or "Do you see Mickey Mouse on that plate?" If you offer him a bite of food and he pushes it away, throws it, or struggles to leave the table, give a warning: "Take a bite or I'll turn your chair away." If he doesn't comply, turn his chair around so that he faces away from the table. This is a form of time-out, and it needs to be brief so he can have a chance to try again soon. Count to yourself to fifteen, ignoring him even if he cries, struggles, or throws things off his tray, then turn him around and present the food again. "Here, take a bite." Do something fun to make it interesting: Try flying it through the air like an airplane heading for the hangar or being silly and telling him, "Eat what I eat." Take a piece of food and hand the same thing to him. Bite yours first and tell him: "Now you take a bite."

If your tactics don't entice your child to stop fussing and struggling, turn his chair around and count to ten—this time to yourself. Turn his chair back to face the table and encourage his interest in eating. Repeat the process again until he complies by at least putting some food in his mouth. To surprise him and possibly cause a break in his fussing, try putting something different on his plate while he is turned around. He may think it was there all along or wonder how it got there. In any case, the novelty may be enough to stop the cycle of misbehavior. If he takes a bite, reinforce it, and decide whether he is likely to continue eating. If not, perhaps you should end the meal while you are ahead. Let him down from the table. Say, "Good eating, John. You can go now." At least you had a few minutes with him at the table, and he knows how to do it now. Keep reinforcing these behaviors at each meal. Before long, you'll have a child who knows what is expected of him when the family sits down to eat.

Nightmares and Sleep Terrors

NIGHTMARES ARE COMMON between the ages of three and five. Just as for adults, they are scary dreams from which a child awakens frightened and fearful. When your child has a nightmare, he may be able to tell you some of its content and feel better if he can share it with you. Accept his fear by sitting with him and offering comfort. Tell him that he had a bad dream, "a story his mind made up in his sleep," but don't be surprised if he has trouble calming down even when he realizes it couldn't be true. If he can't stop thinking about his nightmare, make up a positive ending for him, one in which he uses his cunning to outsmart the demon. Then give him something else to think about, some "happy thoughts" about something fun he once did, his puppy, or a friend. Be careful not to bring up exciting future events that will evoke anticipation and keep him awake longer! Leave his room as soon as he appears settled.

Although most preschool children have a bad dream now and then, frequent nightmares can be a sign that your child is worried or anxious about something. He probably won't recognize or be able to tell you what he is upset about. Just be aware of any changes or problems that might cause him to be insecure, and consult a child psychologist if the problem persists.

Sleep terrors are also common around the age of three, but unlike nightmares, they are not related to dreaming. Sleep terrors happen during the brief, partial wakings that usually occur about one to three hours after a child goes to sleep. Because this involves partially waking from his deepest phase of sleep, a child can become disoriented and confused. Your child may cry out, thrash about on the floor, and push away from or not recognize you when you try to comfort him. He may be difficult to wake, even when talked to or jostled about, and arousing him from a sleep terror is neither necessary nor advised. If you try, he is likely to be confused and frightened when he wakes up. Sleep terrors usually last fifteen minutes to an hour and can be frightening to watch, but there is not much you can do about them. Let your child finish his sleep terror, staying nearby just to make sure he doesn't hurt himself. Use gentle restraint only if needed, as this can increase his agitation. As disruptive and frightening as sleep terrors are to parents who watch them, children typically do not remember them in the morning. Thankfully, they usually occur early in the night while parents are still awake and are typically out-grown by the time a child reaches school age.

Public Misbehavior

MISBEHAVIOR IN THE PRIVACY of your home is one thing; in public, it is quite another. Public misbehavior calls attention to you and your child, and can instantly make you feel that you are an inadequate parent. Your best tactic, of course, is pre-vention. The more clear, consistent expectations you have for your child's behavior at home, the more likely he will behave well in public, but this is not guaranteed. In public, he may sense your hesitation or not know how time-out will work. Without a chair or his room to go to, he may not think your follow-through is possible. He may not know you mean busi-ness until he has experienced time-out in public a time or two. No matter how "in control" your child is at home, a public place is a novel, interesting setting, and a great place to test the limits. Even if you haven't mastered time-out at home yet, if your rules aren't followed, you must follow through with dis-cipline immediately, even in public.

Don't allow your child to do behaviors in public that you do not allow in your home. Your child will sense your hesitation to take charge, and his behavior will be harder to change in the future. Using Progressive Discipline in a grocery store or restau-rant is a good way to stress your rules and show your child that you mean business. In fact, your rules in public places may actu-ally be a little tougher than they are at home: You want your child to stay near your side, eat at the table, not pull things off shelves, and stay relatively quiet. In short, you want him to behave as safely and responsibly as he can at his young age. So what can you do when your child's behavior begins to get out of hand?

If your child is fussy or uncooperative in public, consider:

◆ Is this a case of bad timing? Is she tired? Is she hungry? Sometimes you can't help being in public during these times, but planning around naps and mealtimes can help.

◆ Is your child bored? Can you give him something to do or to play with? What about your keys? A pencil and paper?

◆ Are you expecting him to entertain himself longer than he can at his age? You may need to spend a few minutes playing with or distracting him.

◆ Is his behavior really that bad? How much is your embarrassment playing into your frustration and anger at your child? Many of the people watching you have had similar experiences themselves and are sympathetic. You most likely are bothered by your child's behavior more than other people are. Sometimes parents feel extra pressure when they go out in public with their young child and react to behaviors that don't really require intervention.

Much misbehavior that eventually could turn into a tantrum can be stopped if you anticipate your child's frustration level. Try giving him something new to focus his attention on—your keys, a spoon from the table, a can from the shelf to carry around with him. Entertain him a little and distract him from his frustration. Look for any opportunity to reinforce his appropriate behavior.

Minor misbehavior can often be handled with redirection and a warning that a consequence will be coming if it continues. But blatant misbehavior or a full-blown temper tantrum requires that you use time-out right there on the spot—in a store, in a restaurant, wherever you happen to be.

At age three, one of my children decided she didn't want to try on a sweater I was considering buying her at the store. I held out the sleeve for her to slip her arm into. "No," she said. I held it closer. She ran in the other direction.

"I'll let her go," I thought. "She'll notice I'm not following and stop."

But I was wrong. She rounded the corner out of the children's department and was gone. I immediately took off at a trot, passing surprised shoppers on both sides of the aisle. I saw her heading into the junior women's department, and when I caught up to her, I checked my anger and my fear. I held both her shoulders and turned her to face me. Firmly, I said, "Don't ever run away from Mommy like that. You can get lost where I can't find you." Then I sat her down right there among the sports coats. "Time-out," I said. "You sit here until I say you can get up."

She let out a wail that could be heard in the jewelry department, and several shoppers who were casually walking by stopped to see what I was doing. I waited for her to take a breath, which broke her crying briefly, and told her she could get up. After she calmed down, I talked to her on the way back to the sweater rack. "You scared Mommy. Don't take off like that again." As we neared the girls' department, I said cheerfully, "Let's try this again." I held out the sweater and waited for her to put her arm into the sleeve. Instead, she backed away from me, poised to run again. "If you run from me," I said, "we'll go home without buying anything."

She ran anyway. This time I caught up with her before she reached the corner. "I told you not to run," I said. "Now we have to go home." Without another word, I picked her up in one arm, her jacket in the other, and went down two escalators to the car. Her crying and the looks of people I passed embarrassed me, but I ignored both. In the car, her tantrum vanished. She seemed not to care that I had taken her from the store, but later that night she told my husband, "Mommy didn't buy me anything at the store." It wasn't necessary for me to embarrass her by telling her naughty act to my husband right then. She had gotten the point. The natural consequences had been enough.

"Yes, we had to leave early," I said. "But I bet next time we go, we can find a sweater you like."

And that was the end of it. It was over, and she was back to square one with me. But she never ran away from me in a store again. Any time I would say, "If you don't stop, I'll take you home," she straightened up immediately. That episode taught her that I was prepared to follow through with my threat.

Using Progressive Discipline in a store where people may be watching takes fortitude and determination. You must stick to your beliefs and techniques, even if it is embarrassing at the time. Remember that anyone with children has probably had a similar experience.

Riding in the Car

TO SOME CHILDREN, riding in a car seat is the worst thing that could happen. It means that toys are out of reach, parents are sitting in the front, and it is next to impossible to explore the environment. This kind of restriction is enough to start any child squirming and fussing, which in turn tempts parents to let their child out of the car seat just to keep him quiet. Don't do it. It is a proven fact that car seats save lives. Your child should be buckled in whenever you are driving, even if you are only going a short distance. (Remember that infants should be placed in rear-facing car seats in the backseat, away from airbags.) The best way to get a child to relax in his car seat is to have him use it from the time he is a baby, every time he is in the car, and never change the expectation that he will sit in it. Bending the rules even once in a while can make the problem worse: Taking your child out tells him that struggling can mean freedom. If you do it once, he will struggle harder and longer the next time you want him to stay in his seat.

There will inevitably be times when your child does not want to get into his car seat, particularly if he has a difficult temperament. If he starts out moody or out of sorts, having to be confined this way will make his attitude worse. Don't be discouraged or angry at his show of independence, and don't give in. Put up with his protests—and arched back and wiggling—and consider these ways to make the process go more smoothly:

+ Your Baby or Crawler will struggle least if you start the process in the house. Try using a car seat that is designed to be carried to the car and strapped into place.

+ Offer your Walker, Talker, or Three a choice of items he can take with him in the car. "Do you want to play with your stuffed animal or your truck?" Such choices will help him focus him on playing with one of them and may end his struggle—at least long enough to get the trip underway. Remember that the choice he is to make is *what* to take in the car, not *whether* to sit in the car seat. After he chooses a toy, tell him, "Sit in your seat first; *then* I will give it to you."

◆ Do not move the car until all belts are fastened, including yours. Lead by example: When you buckle up, your child will see that wearing a restraint is a natural behavior, not something you impose only on him.

◆ If necessary, have one parent ride in the backseat to entertain him, but remember that your child will expect you to continue this if you start.

◆ Use toys that he won't lose on the floor easily. Secure a toy with a suction cup to his seat or the car window or look in the store for the kind that attaches directly to a seat belt. Put toys in the pocket behind the front seat where your child can reach them. Have a fresh stash you can reach for when these hit the floor.

◆ On the seat next to your child's car seat, place a box about the size used to store file folders. This can serve as a container for items of entertainment, a surface on which to play with toys, or a fun object to decorate with crayons.

◆ Play song tapes and read-along stories, especially on long trips. Make up new words to the songs based on the things you see as you drive along.

◆ On long trips, stop frequently for rest breaks. Try not to get upset if your itinerary isn't being met.

When your child inevitably discovers that he can wriggle his way out of his car seat or unfasten his own seat belt, you will need to take quick action. Explain that everyone needs to wear a seat belt to keep safe and that you expect him to sit with his on. If he tries to get out of his seat, tell him to sit down and direct his attention to an activity or game. If he succeeds in getting out of his seat or unfastening his belt, say, "You need to stay in your seat." Stop the car safely on the side of the road or in a parking lot, and add, "The car won't go if you are out of your seat." Then get out of the car or turn around in your seat and fasten him back into his. Once he is secured, distract him with talk about where you are headed: "Let's get to the store to buy milk," "Let's get home so we can eat lunch," or "Grandpa is waiting for us." Or give him something novel to do that you brought for such difficult situations. Say, "Sit in your seat and you can color this picture" or "Here's a toy you haven't seen for a while." Start the car only when he sits compliantly in his seat and praise him for behaving appropriately: "I like the way you are sitting in your car seat. That's the way to be safe."

If at age three or older your child does not stay in his car seat even though you stop the car each time he climbs out, tell him he will go to time-out when he gets home if he gets out again. Time-out can be done by having him stay in the car for a few minutes extra at the end of the trip *if this isn't fun and reinforcing for him.* Then let him out of the car and remind him of the rule about staying in his car seat while the car is moving. At the start of the next trip, remind him that the car will stop if he gets out of his seat and that he will stay in the car in time-out when you get where you are going. Help him comply with your request by entertaining and praising him, and by keeping your trips brief at first.

Threes, and some Talkers, are old enough to get into disagreements about who is going to sit where in the car. Your child may want to sit in the front seat, but for children under the age of twelve, the backseat is safest even if the car does not have airbags. Most children will want a seat by a window and will avoid the middle seat (the "hump," as we used to call it) at all cost. Your job is to decide who gets which seat before a fight breaks out. Try a simple rotation system to decide who gets the desired seat. Put each child's name on a separate index card and keep the cards in a stack in the glove box or tray. Each time you get into the car, allow the child whose name is on top to ride in the "best" seat (or to choose which seat to sit in) and place his or her card on the bottom of the stack. This simple way of keeping track ends discussion about whose turn it is and whether your decision is "fair."

Safety

MANY ACCIDENTS INVOLVING children can be prevented with careful arrangement of the environment. Rather than punishing your child for touching things he shouldn't play with, put away as many of these items as possible. If you make sure they are secured, you won't have to constantly correct your child for getting into them. The following list of household and yard hazards includes some common problems to avoid, but it is not comprehensive. Look over your child's environment for other sources of danger and consult your physician if you have questions.

Indoor Safety Check

1. Block off open staircases with gates, sheets of plywood, or Plexiglas. If you use a clear material, put stickers on it so your child will know it is there. Be sure the barricade can't fall in either direction when pushed on, that it has no sharp edges, and that it doesn't pose a fire hazard.
2. Cover electrical outlets with heavy furniture and plug the unused ones with commercial safety plugs. Tape excess cords to the floor to prevent tripping, and repair frayed wires.

3. Unplug and move small appliances like hair dryers and curling irons to a place where they will not tempt little hands. When in use, keep cords away from counter edges.
4. Remove chemicals and toxic products from reach and put safety latches on cabinets and doors.
5. Tape down or remove any loose rugs.
6. Remove toys and other objects that are less than two inches in diameter, or those having small parts. Don't give your small child food items that can be choked on, like hot dogs, grapes, candy, ice, gum, raw carrots, or nuts.
7. Keep plastic bags well out of reach.
8. Use only Mylar, not rubber, balloons to prevent suffocation or choking on the pieces if it pops. Remove strings, or cut them very short to avoid risk of strangulation.
9. Remove tablecloths that could be used to pull dishes or silverware off tables.
10. Keep heavy items and hot pans away from the edge of counters or stoves. Use the back burners and turn pan-handles inward.
11. Turn your water heater down to 120–125°F to avoid burns in the sink or bathtub.
12. Keep the oven and dishwasher doors shut to avoid bumps and burns.
13. Remove plants that are toxic if eaten, including poinsettia, dieffenbachia, and others.
14. Be sure your refrigerator, freezer, and clothes dryer can be opened easily from the inside, and supervise children so they do not play near them.
15. Keep tools, knives, and scissors out of reach or in a locked drawer, and watch for sharp edges on common items such as tape dispensers and plastic wrap boxes.
16. Tie up cords on miniblinds to avoid risk of strangulation.

17. Cushion sharp corners on counters, tables, or fireplace hearths. Put your coffee table away for a few months or pad it to avoid injuries.
18. Keep bathrooms off-limits and do not leave water in the bathtub, spa, or sink. Drowning can occur in less than an inch of water if a child gets stuck.
19. Use only cribs with rails that are two and three-eighths inches apart. Lay your infant on his back in the bed, not on his stomach. Do not place your infant on a waterbed or beanbag chair for risk of suffocation, and be cautious about too-soft pillows or comforters as well.
20. Be extra careful if you use poisons or baits for indoor pests. Contact your county extension agent for recommendations of low-toxic options.

Outdoor Safety Check

1. Don't trust that your child "knows" not to go into the street. He may stay near you when you are outside, but keep your eye on him: He could see something interesting on the other side of the street and take off.
2. Thankfully, child abductions aren't frequent. However, they do occur. Keep your child in sight whenever he is outside. Talk to him about staying away from strangers unless you are present. Role-play or use dolls to show him how to shout "No" and run away if he is approached, and remind him that strangers aren't always strange looking.
3. Survey your yard for any containers that could catch rainwater and pose a risk of drowning. Supervise your child around swimming pools or fishponds.
4. Look for holes that could trap a child or piles of dirt or sand that could cause a slide and risk suffocation.
5. If your yard is unfenced, watch for animals that could frighten or harm your child.

6. Lock away lawn and garden chemicals, and do not let your child play in the yard after fertilizer has been spread. Be aware of neighbors' yards being sprayed—one good gust of wind and your child could be coated.

7. Be extremely cautious about using pesticides and herbicides in your yard. Young children are always in contact with your lawn and other yard surfaces. Whenever possible, use products that biodegrade rapidly and have no known toxic effect on humans.

8. Check for plants in your yard that may be poisonous when touched or eaten.

9. Lock your garage or shed to block access to tools, chemicals, paints, or mower.

Saying "Please" and "Thank You"

CHILDREN CANNOT BE expected to reliably say "please" and "thank you" until well into their school years. However, this behavior can be encouraged and reinforced beginning in the Talker stage.

> ◆ Modeling the use of the words "please" and "thank you" for your child can be extremely important in teaching him to use them. Watching you and hearing your tone of voice will help him know when they are appropriate and expected. Say "please" and "thank you" often to other children and adults as well as your child.
>
> ◆ Look for books that can show your child when it is appropriate to say "please" and "thank you."
>
> *(continued)*

◆ When your child wants something—like a glass of milk—pause for him to say "Please." If he doesn't, model it for him by saying matter-of-factly, "May I have a glass of milk, *please?*" Your child will mimic your statement in the tone of voice you said it, and you will have taught him the appropriate way to make a request. Use this modeling procedure whenever your child makes requests of other people, as well.

◆ When you do something for your child and he forgets to say "Thank you," say it out loud as if talking to yourself: "Thank you, Mom (or Dad)." Wait for your child to repeat your comment. If he doesn't, don't force the issue; just hearing you say it for him will help him learn the appropriate time to thank you. Eventually, he will say it spontaneously.

Sharing

PRIOR TO AGE THREE, most children don't interact a lot with other children, at least not to the point of sharing with them. True sharing does not begin until children are close to three and understand the concept of possession, "this is yours and this is mine." Even at this age, however, children are still quite egocentric and will not always give up a toy or swing to another child. Learning empathy and social etiquette will take years of practice. The following approaches will help as your child learns these skills:

> ◆ Make your basic rules clear to your child, e.g., "We don't take other people's things," and "We don't hit, bite, push, or hurt other people if they take our things." Remind him of the rules each time you see an inappropriate behavior and use time-out when appropriate.
>
> ◆ When your child wants a toy belonging to someone else, encourage him to offer the other child a different toy in exchange. Say, "See if he wants this instead." If the other child doesn't want to give up his toy, tell your child, "He is playing with that toy. Let's find something else to do." Reinforce his effort to trade and help begin a different activity.
>
> ◆ Look for opportunities to reinforce your child's positive social behaviors. When you see him give another child a toy on his own, be sure to label and praise it: "That was nice sharing. You gave him your toy."
>
> ◆ When waiting for a turn on a slide or merry-go-round, hold your child gently by the hand or shoulders. Tell him, "Wait for your turn. It is her turn now. You will be next." When his turn comes, say, "It's your turn now. Thank you for waiting."

Shopping Trips

BABIES, CRAWLERS, AND WALKERS

Babies, Crawlers, and Walkers can be easy to manage in a store if they visit in a stroller, backpack, or grocery cart. Take toys or food items along to ward off hunger, and diapers for changing, and your child should be able to accompany you for several hours at a time. Give your child something that is safe to hold for you, like toilet tissue or a bag of apples. Busy hands are less likely to reach for things they should not have. If your child can reach the things in your cart when it fills up and persists in pulling things out, try partially filling one cart, leaving it in the front of the store, and starting with a second one. Keep your trip short, put only safe, unbreakable items near your child, and plan to distract and entertain him while you are there.

TALKERS AND THREES

The key to teaching your older child how to act in a store is to take a few short training trips as practice. When you are not in a hurry, you can watch your child's behavior and reinforce small successes in a way that makes later trips much easier. First, take toys along to keep her occupied and something to eat if she gets hungry. Grocery shopping can whet a child's appetite and increase her fussiness. Feed your child ahead of time, or ask the store clerk if you can pay for juice or some crackers after your child has eaten them if you take the bottle or box to the cashier at checkout.

Before you begin shopping, tell your child the rules: Stay with me, touch only what I tell you to touch, and talk in an "indoor voice." You will want to convey to your child that you expect her to behave a certain way, just because you said so, but it is okay to promise a small treat at the end of the trip if she behaves the way you have requested. Offer to buy her a small treat, ride the horse, or give a star on a token chart, but don't make that the focus of your shopping trip. Keep her near you while you shop and make simple requests that can keep her occupied, like, "Put this box in our cart" or "Can you find a can of green beans?" Tell her frequently how well she is doing, and name the specific behaviors you like: "I like how you helped me find the cans I needed" or "You are doing a good job staying near me." Give your child plenty of attention for the behaviors that you want to see happen again.

If your child misbehaves in some significant way, like running away or pulling things off shelves, remind her of the rule, such as, "Stay next to me" or "Touch only what I tell you to touch." Tell her that the next time she does it, she will sit in time-out and not get her treat, then sit her in time-out right there in the aisle the very next time the behavior occurs. If she creates too big a scene, take her to time-out in the car, but don't necessarily go home right away as a consequence. If you don't have a lot of shopping left to do, sit in the car for a few minutes, repeat the rules for her, and tell her you want her to "try again" to behave in the store. Once inside, keep your visit brief, praise her appropriate behaviors, and ignore any requests to provide the specific treat you withdrew. Tell her that she can try again the next time you go to the store.

Sleepwalking

SLEEPWALKING CAN OCCUR as soon as a child is able to walk, and some children are more prone to sleepwalking than others. If your child has done it once, he is likely to do it again. Sleepwalkers have been known to travel to the kitchen or other parts of the house, or even out the front door on occasion. This can be a disturbing problem for parents who need to get some sleep themselves but are worried about keeping their child safe. Scientists used to think people were acting out their dreams during sleepwalking, but they now know that dreaming occurs during a different phase of sleep, a phase when a person typically doesn't move. When your child sleepwalks, he will be difficult to wake, and there is no reason to do so; he can easily be guided back to bed. To know when your sleep-walker is up and about, put a bell or other alarm on his door to alert you when he leaves his room.

Talking on the Phone

ONE YOUNG MOTHER, Pam, asked for help managing her son's demands for attention whenever she talked on the phone. Recently, she had gone into another room to get away from his whining and he cut himself on a glass he pulled off the counter. Pam realized that this wasn't a safe approach to hav-ing a quiet phone conversation, but she didn't know what to do. "No sooner do I say 'hello' but Josh is pulling on my sleeve for attention. I know I should ignore him, but he gets worse and worse until I finally have to put down the phone and holler at him. Then he cries, and I feel guilty. I wish I could get him to stop." As soon as the phone rang, it signaled Josh to begin his begging. Here are some suggestions that helped keep him out of trouble when Pam had to be on the phone:

1. Keep a box of toys on top of your refrigerator or in some other out-of-the-way place, and take it out only when the phone rings. Practice this with a friend a few times so your child will understand that your talking on the phone is his signal to get an otherwise unavailable toy.

2. Take phone calls only when your child is sleep-ing or is engrossed in an activity with friends. Even the most well-behaved child will want your attention soon after you begin a call. Keep calls short and offer to call your friends back later.

3. Tell your child ahead of time that you will have a "special play time" with him as soon as you finish your phone call if he does not interrupt you. Promise to lift him in the air, read him a story, or something else that is fun. As soon as the phone rings (or you begin dialing), remind him of your promise, then follow through when you hang up. At first, keep your calls very brief to insure success. Show him how it will work with a few trial calls from friends.

4. If your child is at least three, try creating a token system just for phone calls. Give him a token every few minutes while you are on the phone and exchange them for a reward when your call is over. Remember to start out with very short calls so he learns how this works.

5. Warn friends or business callers that you may need to interrupt your conversation to redirect your child. Take a moment to find him a toy or activity. If he gets too out of hand, end your phone call and put him in time-out. Call your colleague back when he is quiet again.

Tantrums

TANTRUMS ARE THE HALLMARK of the two-year-old period, but they can happen at younger or older ages as well. They often involve crying, sitting or lying on the floor, kicking, screaming, or hollering angry statements. Some children even hold their breath as they stubbornly refuse to do what is asked. Tantrums can seem to come out of nowhere, but most of the time they derive from frustration and can be predicted at least a few seconds before they start. Perhaps you couldn't get the seatbelt undone or reach a toy he wanted quickly enough, or, worse yet, perhaps you had to say, "No." Sometimes your child's tantrum may have nothing to do with you: He couldn't reach something on the counter, another child took his toy, or the block wouldn't go into the wrong hole.

When a tantrum occurs, it is almost always loud, obnoxious, and inconvenient. Your child is out of control and dealing with frustration in the most basic way possible. Responding quickly and matter-of-factly can stop some behaviors that signal a tantrum is on the way, but a full-blown tantrum cannot always be prevented. If having a tantrum gets your attention— or better yet, gets you to come to the rescue—your child is likely to have a tantrum any time he encounters frustration.

Remember your basic behavioral principles. A behavior is likely to decrease if it does not receive reinforcement. That means the best way to respond to a tantrum is to ignore it. If you try to discuss or reason with your child, he will not hear what you say, and you will reinforce his behavior with your attention. Whenever possible, deal with the tantrum where it occurs, not later when you get home or down the hall in his room. In public places, take your child to the car or a restroom, or grit your teeth and put him in time-out right where he stands, even in the aisle of a grocery store. At home, sit him on the couch or in a chair and walk away. He may follow you just to keep his audience, but don't give in to his tantrum. Getting results will make having tantrums his primary way of dealing with frustration. Do your best to completely ignore what your child is doing or saying (unless he is in danger of hurting himself). If possible, don't talk to your child or even look at him. If you feel that you may lose your temper and yell at or spank your child, this is the time to distance yourself from him. You may even need to go into a different room so you can cool off a little. If you can wait it out, eventually your child will be ready to interact appropriately again. When he quiets, tell him, "Good, you're done crying (or fussing or yelling)," and suggest an activity for him to do. If he doesn't want to do it and starts his tantrum again, ignore it and begin the process over again.

If a tantrum goes on for a long time and shows no sign of stopping, it is possible for you to carefully intervene to hurry the process along, but your timing must be very good so you don't reinforce the tantrum behavior with your attention. Wait for a break in the tantrum, such as when your child pauses to look around or to take a deep breath before wailing again. At that moment say, "Good, you stopped your tantrum." It doesn't really matter whether he intended to stop his tantrum or not; he will probably remain quiet for a few more seconds simply out of surprise. During that pause, quickly introduce something novel that might interest him, like "Your teddy bear is waiting for you in the kitchen." Be careful not to offer a reward that involves your attention; he may do the whole process later just to get to that point again.

Tantrums usually decrease as a child learns more expressive language and is better able to get his point across when he wants something. When he is a little older, he will also be able to be reasoned with, understand that a tantrum is inappropriate, and get himself under control faster when sent to time-out. Tell him, "When you have stopped, you can get up." If the tantrum happened after he was asked to do something, be sure to have him complete the request when he gets up. A child who gets so angry that he throws himself on the ground, bites himself, or bangs his head will rarely hurt himself. These behaviors are done for attention and usually can be ignored. Move him to a safe place and let him calm a little before you intervene.

Thumbsucking

THUMBSUCKING CAN BE a source of comfort to a young child and is not usually considered a problem until five or six years of age. Even then, children usually stop on their own if it is simply ignored. However, your dentist may want you to discourage your child from sucking his thumb before he reaches school age. If your child's thumbsucking is a problem at age three or older, try the following approaches. Focus at first on reducing the amount of time he spends sucking rather than on eliminating it altogether.

◆ Thumbsucking often occurs when children are bored, anxious, or sleepy. Times when they are expected to sit quietly and concentrate present prime opportunities for this habit behavior to occur. Keep your child occupied and offer other things to do when he is likely to start sucking his thumb. Some children reduce their thumbsucking when they are given something to hold or put in their mouth.

◆ Probably the best way to reduce your child's interest in sucking his thumb is to ignore him when he does it and give him praise and attention when he does not. This involves patience and time, since he is not likely to give up this habit quickly. Watch for his thumbsucking, but don't comment on it or tell him to stop. Simply remove any attention or physical contact until he spontaneously takes his thumb out of his mouth. Tell him, "I like the way you took your thumb out" or "You look so nice when your

(continued)

thumb isn't in your mouth!" Use natural opportunities to withdraw reinforcing activities when
he sucks his thumb, with or without commenting on the thumbsucking. If you are reading a
book to him, and he pops his thumb into his
mouth, stop reading without acting irritated or
disgusted. A touch on his arm may remind him
what you are waiting for. Start reading again
when the thumb comes out.

◆ If ignoring thumbsucking and rewarding other
behaviors does not decrease your child's
thumbsucking, try making him aware when he
sucks his thumb. Tell him to stop or remind
him with a gentle touch on the shoulder, back,
or hand.

◆ Ask your child to catch himself before he sucks
his thumb again and to tell you when he stops
on his own. Getting him to notice his behavior
himself may reduce his thumbsucking.

◆ During times when your child is likely to suck
his thumb, when watching television, or just
before bed, challenge him to keep his hand out
of his mouth for fifteen minutes. Reward him
every time a minute goes by and his thumb has
not been in his mouth. Use a token chart if he
is old enough to understand the concept.

Toilet Training

MOST CHILDREN CAN CONTROL their bowel and bladder during the
day by about twenty-eight months of age, but many have day-
time accidents until three or four years of age and nighttime

accidents into their early school years. Children develop control at different times, so don't start toilet training too early. Your child must be ready to learn before you can teach him these skills, and he will usually learn bowel control before controlling urination.

> Wait until he is two years of age and look for these signs that he is ready for toilet training:
>
> ◆ Gives some intentional sign that he needs to go, like pulling at his diaper.
>
> ◆ Hides or grunts when he has a bowel movement.
>
> ◆ Pulls down his own pants.
>
> ◆ Remains dry for two hours during the day and wakes dry from naps.
>
> ◆ Follows simple commands.

When you are ready to begin toilet training your child, be matter-of-fact and supportive. Parents who are too anxious to be free of diapers and messy accidents can forget that children can't learn what they aren't developmentally capable of doing. Techniques must be applied with respect and understanding. Never yell at or humiliate your child for having accidents, and don't compare him to other children.

> ◆ When your child's grunting or the look on his face tells you he is having a bowel movement, use words to describe the event for him. Say, "You are going potty," or "poop" (or whatever words you use at your house). Put him on the potty-chair with his diaper on so he begins to associate the feeling with the right words and place. *(continued)*

◆ If you are comfortable having your child watch you go to the bathroom, allow him to imitate your behavior. Place a potty-chair near the toilet about the time he usually goes and ask him to sit on it. Be sure he is comfortable and that his feet rest flat on the floor. He must feel secure and be able to relax, so don't force him to sit down. If he resists, wait a week or so before trying again; you won't want him to associate the potty-chair with a struggle.

◆ Praise your child whenever he sits on the potty-chair cooperatively, and make a big deal out of anything he produces in it. Let him help you pour the contents into the "big potty," but wait to flush it. Some children are frightened by noise, and others are upset to see the thing they produced disappear down the toilet.

◆ Have your child sit on the potty after lunch, after supper, and before bedtime, and as frequently as once per hour during the rest of the day to catch her before she goes in her diaper. Again, do not force the issue if she resists or respond with anger to accidents. Praise her for trying whenever she sits on the potty, and cheer her successes.

◆ Since your child will be two or three when you are doing this, a reward chart may be useful, as it will give you a way to reinforce the proper behaviors. This chart must be simple and convenient, and should focus on the behaviors that lead up to using the potty correctly. Make a couple of charts with ten squares on them for stars. Keep one with you when you go out and

(continued)

the other on the door in the bathroom. Make frequent checks in the bathroom for "dry pants" and give a star each time you catch him without a soiled diaper. Tell him he can earn another star for peeing or pooping in the potty, if he wants to try (or for sitting on the potty, if he is reluctant to try). When the card is filled, give him a small reward like a book, ball, or sticker to wear on his shirt and begin a new chart. Keep the chart you use for going in public restrooms separate so you can use it on the spot, and don't forget to use it.

◆ When your child has used the potty successfully several times, tell him you think he is ready for underpants. Be excited with him and try not to go back to diapers unless he has many accidents after the switch. Have him wear several pairs of underpants for a while if it will help to avoid going back to diapers. If you do need to go back, do so without shaming him or appearing disappointed.

Waking Up

MORNING CAN BE A TOUGH time to get up and going, even for adults, and some people have more difficulty than others do. As a parent, you will have at least a small role in determining how your child will approach the new day and other people in it by the way you treat him when he wakes. Here are some ways to help with this tough transition:

◆ Watch your mood and voice tone in the morning. If you sound irritated and gruff, your child will respond the same way. Take a few minutes to set the right tone; wake him with a hug instead of bright lights and hollering. Hold him for a moment, and take the opportunity to tell him you love him and think he's a great kid.

◆ Capitalize on any novel or interesting activity the day promises. Introduce them subtly when you wake him by asking, "Are you ready to have scrambled eggs?" or "Will Joey be at the center today?"

◆ Some children wake easily. Others may need more encouragement and effort from you. This is just an individual difference, not lack of cooperation. Give yourself time for extra reminders or assistance if your child is not a morning person.

◆ If your child is crabby and yells at you, tell him you don't like being treated that way and walk out of the room. Come back in a few minutes with a cheerful voice and offer to help him, but leave the room briefly again if he continues to treat you inappropriately.

◆ Be sure to reinforce your child when he wakes up in a good mood. Tell him you like the way he is behaving. Some people will call an uncooperative child crabby or lazy, which promotes a negative self-image. It gives the message that the child is always expected to be that way. On a good morning, try telling your child something positive about himself, like, "You are such a morning person! I like the way you smile in the morning." This promotes a much better self-image than calling him lazy or crabby.

(continued)

> ◆ Lay your child's clothes out the night before and limit his access to more than a few choices. Let him wear the clothes he decides on, even if they are a little odd in combination. Day-care personnel and other parents are very sympathetic to the whimsical choices of a young child. Just smile and tell them you are pleased that he dressed himself that morning.

Wanting to Sleep with You

BABIES AND CRAWLERS

Babies and Crawlers are not able to think about requesting to sleep with their parents, and allowing them to fall asleep in your bed usually does not present a problem. However, toward the end of the Crawler stage, this can easily become a requirement for your child to go to sleep if you allow it to continue. Be cautious about lying down with your child or bringing him into bed with you at this age or it may be difficult to stop later.

WALKERS, TALKERS, AND THREES

Children learn very young that it can be more fun and comfortable to sleep with a parent, and once they can get out of their bed, they often climb into their parents' bed during the night. Although some parents find it convenient and cozy to let their child sleep in their bed, allowing this behavior can be a problem for many reasons. First, it interferes with a child's ability to self-comfort and sleep on his own. Second, it often puts a strain on the parents' relationship. Finally, it can be difficult to stop. Don't allow this behavior at some times and not others. Occasional reinforcement—like getting to sleep in a parent's bed every now and then—can make a behavior harder to extinguish when you decide you have had enough. If you are already allowing your child to sleep in your bed, plan to make a change as soon as possible, but be prepared for some sleepless nights while you do it.

Tell your child that she can only get into your bed if it is daylight out. Most Talkers and Threes can distinguish light from darkness and understand when it is morning. At night, everyone should sleep in her own bed. If your child is used to having you around for comfort when she wakes in the middle of the night, she will probably come looking for you. Without expressing anger, take her back to her room, tuck her in, and say, "Good night. See you in the morning." Force yourself to stay awake for a few minutes to be sure she doesn't sneak into your room and climb back into your bed unnoticed. Return her to her bed every time she gets out. If you are likely to not hear her when she heads your way, put a bell or buzzer on the frame of her door to alert you when she leaves her room.

It can be tough to say "no" when your child asks to sleep in your bed. When one of my children was three years old, she woke during the night, said it was too dark in her room, and insisted on sleeping in ours. I decided to convince her that this wasn't a good idea.

"It's dark in our room, too," I told her, but she begged and begged to join us. "Wait here," I said. "Let me check with your dad." In our room, we plotted our response. He would lie still with his back to us, and I would orchestrate the rest. I warned her that we both move a lot in our sleep and I wasn't sure how comfortable she would be, but she brought her stuffed raccoon and climbed in. As soon as I lay down, I rolled over and pushed her gently between my husband's back and mine.

"You're squishing me!" she said.

"Sorry," I said. "I roll around a lot when I am going to sleep."

I said good night and proceeded to do the same thing again. After a few minutes of this, she announced: "I'm sleeping in my own room. You guys are too squishing for me!" In the morning, she bounced into our room to join us, but she never asked to sleep in our room again.

Whining and Begging

MOST CHILDREN WHINE, some more than others do. Whining is a natural behavior when a child is tired or wants something he can't have, and unfortunately, it often gets results from parents. Children don't truly know how annoying whining is, and many times they can't recognize they are doing it or stop when they are told to quit. However, when parents give in just to get their child to stop, the child learns that whining is all it takes to get what he wants. If you don't want to give your child something he desires, say, "No," and give a brief reason. Tell him it doesn't belong to him or that he can have it the next time, later, or after dinner, but don't give it to him when he is whining. Try directing his attention to other things. If you had planned to provide whatever he is whining for, don't do it while he is throwing a tantrum. He needs to learn that the word "no" means "no," and that "wait" means the desired object will be available when he stops. Distract him and ignore any further begging. Call his attention to something else so that he stops briefly and you aren't responding immediately to his whining. Walk him into the next room, pointing out different objects, then return and say, "What were you asking for? A cookie? Say 'Cookie, please.' Good!"

When your child makes his request in a whiny tone, tell

him "No whining." Ask him to use a different voice. For example, tell him to "say it nicely," and demonstrate asking for it without whining. When he says it appropriately, give it to him right away if he can have it. Otherwise, repeat his request again in the "right" tone of voice, "Can I have it please?" If the answer is "No," say so, and don't give in.

An older child can be helped to understand that he needs to stop begging in order to get what he is asking for. Tell him, "When you are quiet for a minute, I will give it to you, but not if you are whining." Then wait for him to quiet down. If you can't give him what he wants and distraction doesn't work, look at the section on tantrums (page 221).

Sometimes changing your perspective helps manage a whining problem. This worked for one parent who had found his child's behavior very frustrating. His daughter, Ella, whined most often when her brother was around. When her brother did anything that might take her father's attention from her, Ella would fuss to her father: "Danny's bothering me!" Often, this resulted in her father saying, "Ella, stop whining," at which point her whining would escalate. After this went on for several minutes, Ella would become aggressive toward her brother, hitting him or taking his toys, and end up in time-out. Simple distraction early in Ella's sequence of behaviors might have been effective at getting her behavior to subside, but her father had difficulty doing it because of his anger at her whining. He needed a way to not have her behaviors annoy him so much. As strange as it sounds, I suggested that this father try treating her whining as a "gift" rather than misbehavior—a gift that told him she wanted and valued his attention. I told him, "Every time Ella whines this week, respond as though she just said to you, 'Daddy, here's a flower I picked for you.'" He was to respond without anger, as though it was a flower, and direct her to a more appropriate activity. If it were a flower, he'd probably say, "Go see if there's a vase under the sink" or "Let's put it in this glass." When she whined, he learned to say, "Ella, look in that drawer over there and see if that toy is still there," or "Come help me stir this soup." As far-fetched as this may sound, this father learned to respond to his daughter's whining as though she had asked for attention in a more appropriate way, and he found it much easier to give another task to distract her. Eventually, Ella learned to go right to other activities when her brother started to bother her, without having to be directed there.

Epilogue

Throughout this book, you have been asked to think about your long-term parenting goals, the principles of behavior management, and parenting as a process rather than a series of problems that must be fixed. Your concern for your child will never end, but your role as her protector and teacher will last a relatively short time in her life. You will want to give her the tools she needs to go forth in the world treating others well and being treated well by them. So much of how your child will behave she will learn from watching you. She will learn from the way you treat her, the way you treat others, and the way you manage stress. However you would like your child to behave, you must first do the same around her, for you are her primary teacher. Having that responsibility isn't always easy, or welcomed. Parenting can be a struggle for a few hours—and challenging for years to come—but it will be worth the effort if you do it right. If you parent with commitment, respect, trustworthiness, and good technique, your child will learn those skills, too, and your parenting will be successful. In the short term you will have a child who behaves well much of the time and learns to think about what she is doing; in the long term, she will "pass it on" to others she meets—perhaps even to her own children some day. Don't give up when the going gets tough. If you can keep your parenting goals in mind through tantrums, squabbles, and food on the floor, the rest will take care of itself.